MIRACLES AND REVELATIONS

During the Divine Liturgy

MIRACLES AND REVELATIONS

During the Divine Liturgy

Compiled by
Holy Monastery of the Paraclete
Oropos, Attica, Greece

Uncut Mountain Press

MIRACLES AND REVELATIONS
During the Divine Liturgy

Uncut Mountain Press
Florence, AZ
uncutmountainpress.com

+1 (520) 895-1804 | info@uncutmountainpress.com

Scriptural quotations are taken from the KJV. For the Old Testament, where the KJV differs from the Greek, quotations are from Sir Lancelot Brenton's translation of the Septuagint. Quotations from the Psalms are taken from *The Psalter According to the Seventy* by Holy Transfiguration Monastery in Brookline, MA. Quotations from the liturgical texts of the Church are likewise taken from the translations of Holy Transfiguration Monastery.

Images are from Uncut Mountain Supply or in the public domain unless cited otherwise.

The first English translation and publication of this collection of texts was undertaken by Fr. Ermolaos Iatrou from the nineteenth edition of the Holy Monastery of the Paraclete, Oropos, Attica, in Greece. This second English edition presents a text thoroughly edited and revised by Uncut Mountain Press.

Miracles and Revelations During the Divine Liturgy—2nd English ed.
Compiled by the Holy Monastery of the Paraclete.
Translated and edited by Uncut Mountain Press.

ISBN (softcover): 978-1-63941-087-3
ISBN (ebook): 978-1-63941-088-0

I. Eastern Orthodox Church
II. Eastern Orthodox Spirituality

Printed in Canada.

"The mystery needs no treatment; rather, it is proclaimed only as being what it is… It is revealed not by wisdom but by the Holy Spirit, inasmuch as we are able to receive it."

— St. John Chrysostom
(as quoted in the Introduction)

CONTENTS

PUBLISHER'S NOTE

The publication of this book is largely due to the work and encouragement of a dear friend and outstanding modern Orthodox missionary to Africa, the ever-memorable Fr. Ermolaos Iatrou. Father Ermolaos worked absolutely tirelessly to bring the Gospel and the Faith to the far reaches of the African continent, including arranging for the first translation and edition of this book, which he asked us to perfect and publish for English speakers in North America.

Father Ermolaos was exceptional in many ways, not least of all as one of a very few married clergymen who has his family in the missionary field. He was largely responsible for the establishment and tremendous growth of the Orthodox Church in Malawi, where he built the Church of Saint Nektarios, and many other churches, with the help of many young men whom he had catechized and guided to the priesthood. He was their father, their inspiration, and he nurtured a generation of African clergymen who now serve the Orthodox Church with zeal.

Father Ermolaos was a rare clergyman for another reason. He strove to follow with exactitude the Holy Fathers, eschewing every innovation and heresy of our day with great boldness. His principled stand on matters of Faith led him to other missionary outposts. Having overcome grave illness during the time of the so-called pandemic, he

Father Ermolaos Iatrou

continued his mission undeterred, moving to the yet-to-be touched missionary field of Liberia, to extend the Light of Orthodoxy to new souls.

It was there, in the midst of his holy work, that the Lord called him suddenly to the heavenly realm on the first of April 2022. All who knew him mourned his loss even as they remember his zeal and love for the Incarnate Truth with gratitude and reverence. He offered not only his last bit of strength for the Gospel but also his learning, generously entrusting to us translations of spiritual classics such as this, that the treasures of the Faith might enrich many others.

May the sacrifice, love, zeal and missionary spirit of the ever-memorable Fr. Ermolaos continue to inspire all who encounter his work and the fruit of his labors. Memory Eternal, dear Father Ermolaos!

Father Ermolaos Iatrou

St. John Chrysostom (mosaic from the 11th century)
Saint Sophia Cathedral, Kiev

Introduction

The Christian's life in the Church is a continuous mystery. From the day of his baptism, his existence is organically tied to the central person of the Church, the God-man Jesus Himself. His journey with the Saviour Christ becomes a high and ineffable mystery.

This mystical relationship reaches its peak in the Divine Eucharist which is accomplished within the Divine Liturgy. This is the supreme and most dread mystery of our Church.

Here, incomprehensibly yet truly, the bread and the wine, which man offers God as symbols of his own life, are changed, "by the power and activity of the All-Holy Spirit," into the Body and Blood of Christ. The faithful partakes of this Body and Blood of the Master with a pure conscience "unto the remission of sins and unto life everlasting," receiving the whole Godhead within him. For as He said, "he that eateth my flesh and drinketh my blood abideth in me and I in him" (John 5:65). For this reason after Divine Communion the Christians can confess, "We and Christ are one" (Saint John Chrysostom).

This theanthropic communion is realized in the common celebration of all heavenly and earthly creatures. In every divine liturgy, gathered around the holy altar, are the All-Holy Theotokos, All Saints, the angelic world, our brothers living and fallen asleep, the entire creation. United they concelebrate the liturgy and together they glorify God for the manifestation of His love toward the world.

Thus have the people of God lived the divine mystagogy throughout the course of the centuries. Today's Christian experiences this same reality, according to the measure of his faith and spiritual struggle. In fact, sometimes God allows the veil that covers what is being done in the Divine Liturgy to be lifted, and then the great mystery is revealed, not "through a glass, darkly," but "in very deed." Then again, at other times, Divine Communion itself is seen associated with strange and marvelous signs, palpable, astonishing miracles.

Through all the visible activities of the sacred mysteries, God—in accordance with the circumstance and His unsearchable will—intervenes and heals diseases, saves from dangers, rewards the virtuous, strengthens the fighters, supports those of little faith, rouses the sluggards, reproves the sinners, leads men to the Truth of the Church…

In the pages that follow, the reader will find a small collection of such wondrous interventions and revelations related to the Divine Liturgy and Divine Communion.

The accounts were collected from various sources, of which the main ones are numbered at the end of the book. The numbers noted in brackets at the end of each account refer to these sources.

To the many noteworthy things that are written and preached in our days having as their aim the liturgical renaissance of the Church's fulness, we humbly add this book too; and we believe that in its own way it will lead to the "miracle of the mysteries"—provided that it be read with simplicity and with the respect that is fitting for what our Church's tradition has preserved. Besides, "the mystery needs no treatment; rather, it is proclaimed only as being what it is… It is revealed not by wisdom but by the Holy Spirit, inasmuch as we are able to receive it" (Saint John Chrysostom).

HOLY MONASTERY OF THE PARACLETE

PART I

THE POWER OF THE MYSTERY

Christ flanked by the Virgin Mary and
Saint John the Baptist in supplication

The Bread That Turned to Stone

During the time of St. John Chrysostom (4th century), there lived a wealthy man who, together with his wife, adhered to the heresy of Macedonius. One day, after hearing the saint's teaching, the man repented and returned to the truth of the One, Holy, Catholic, and Apostolic Church. His wife, however, while confessing the Orthodox faith outwardly, inwardly continued to cling to her heretical beliefs.

On a major feast day of the Church, when many Christians customarily received Holy Communion, the following incident occurred:

The wife secretly went to receive communion from the heretical clergy. However, she did not consume the bread, but instead gave it to her servant to hide, without anyone noticing.[1]

Later that day, she went to the Orthodox church with her husband to receive Holy Communion. When her turn came, she took the Holy Bread from the hand of St. John Chrysostom, but did not place it in her mouth. Instead, she

1 In the early centuries, Christians received the Holy Gifts separately. First, they would receive the Holy Bread in their right palm, and then partake of the consecrated Wine from the Holy Chalice. This practice continues today for clergy who commune within the sanctuary. For the rest of the faithful, the simultaneous reception of the Holy Gifts with the Holy Spoon was implemented, likely after the 8th century.

secretly consumed the bread she had received earlier from the heretics.

Immediately, she was struck by a miracle: the heretical bread turned into stone in her mouth!

Terrified, she cried out and confessed the entire incident to those present. From that moment, she wholeheartedly believed in the Orthodox Church.

St. John Chrysostom took the stone and placed it in the sacristy as a permanent witness to the miracle.

[22]

The Prayer of the Anaphora

In the region of Apamea, Syria's second province, there was a village called Gonagon. Once, about a mile away from the village, some children were tending their animals. While playing, they agreed among themselves to perform the Divine Liturgy, imitating what they had seen the priest do in church. They appointed one of them as a "priest" and two others as "deacons." Then, they approached a smooth rock, where they placed bread and a clay vessel filled with wine, as if on an altar.

The "priest" stood in the middle, with the "deacons" on his right and left. He began reciting the Prayer of the Anaphora,[2] while the "deacons" fanned with their kerchiefs

2 The Prayer of the Anaphora is recited dialogically between the priest and the congregation during the most central part of the Divine Liturgy, known as the Holy Anaphora, which begins after the recitation of the Symbol of Faith (the Nicene Creed). This prayer includes the apostolic blessing, thanksgiving, the hymn of victory, the commemoration of the Lord's redemptive work, the proclamation of the words instituting the mystery of the Holy Eucharist, the invocation of the Holy Spirit for the sanctification of

in place of liturgical fans.[3] The young "priest" knew the Prayer of the Anaphora because he often stood, like all children, in front of the holy sanctuary during the sacred services, listening and learning the prayers.

After everything had been done according to the ecclesiastical order and as they were preparing to break the bread, something terrifying happened: Fire fell from heaven and turned to ashes everything they had put forth as offerings, and even the rock itself. Not the slightest trace remained!

The children, terrified, fell to the ground and remained there half-dead, unable to utter a word. The parents became worried about their delay. Searching, they found them in this state and brought them back to the village. They persistently asked to learn the cause of their shock, but received no answer.

Later, when the children recovered, they recounted what they had done and experienced. Soon, the bishop was informed of the miraculous event. He went with all the clergy to the site of the miracle and saw the marks of the heavenly fire. Then he placed the children in a monastery. While on the site of the fire, he built a church and around it a beautiful monastery.

[25]

the Holy Gifts, the commemoration of the living and the departed (diptychs), and the final blessing.

3 The litrguical fans [*ripidia*] were special fans made of leather or feathers, which the deacons held during the Divine Liturgy and waved over the Holy Gifts to prevent any insects from falling into the Holy Chalice.

The Necessity of Holy Communion

An Egyptian man, known for his dissolute life, became infatuated with a married and virtuous woman. Unable to seduce her, he turned to a sorcerer, asking him to drive the woman away from her husband.

When the sorcerer failed to affect the woman's mind, he used his dark arts to make her appear as a mare. Her husband, devastated, saw what appeared to be a horse that neither ate nor spoke for three days.

Desperate, he placed a halter on her and brought her to Saint Macarius.

"Why have you brought a mare here?" asked the astonished monks near the saint's cell.

"She is my wife," the man replied. "She has fasted for three days and does not speak. Somehow, she has been transformed."

The monks informed the saint, who said, "You are the ones with horse-like eyes. She is a woman, just as she was created."

Then, St. Macarius blessed water, poured it over her head, and prayed. Immediately, she appeared as a woman to all.

After feeding her, the saint gave the husband counsel. Turning to the woman, he said, "Never again absent yourself from the Church, nor distance yourself from Holy Communion. This happened to you because you had not partaken of the Immaculate Mysteries for five weeks."

[40, 46]

Saint Tychon and the Grapes

St. Tychon, Bishop of Amathus in Cyprus (4th–5th century), was a renowned wonderworker. Among his many miracles is the following:

St. Tychon, Bishop of Amathus, Cyprus (18th century icon), Yaroslavl, Russia

One day, vineyard workers were planting in a field. A laborer threw aside some dried vine branches, believing them useless. The saint took one such branch and, after praying and invoking the Holy Trinity, planted it in the ground.

To the amazement of all, the dry branch took root, sprouted, blossomed, and produced sweet, ripe grapes—months before the usual harvest.

From then on, this miracle repeated yearly. On June 16, the feast of St. Tychon, the vine produces ripe grapes, which are distributed to the faithful as a blessing. For many years after his death, the grapes remained green and sour until the Divine Liturgy of the feast began. Then they would gradually darken and sweeten.

By the end of the service, the grapes became black and exceedingly sweet. Those who partook of them felt physical well-being and deep spiritual peace. To this day, those who honor the saint continue to experience this miracle.

[22, 41]

The Miracle of Orthodoxy

About thirty miles from Aegae in Cilicia, two stylite ascetics lived in separate hermitages—one Orthodox and the other a follower of the Severian heresy. The heretic persistently tried to convince the Orthodox ascetic to accept his views.

The Orthodox stylite, seeking to reveal the truth, asked the heretic to send him a portion of his communion.

Believing the Orthodox ascetic would embrace his heresy, the heretic sent a portion. The Orthodox ascetic boiled water in a cauldron and cast the heretical portion into it—it immediately dissolved.

Then he placed a portion of the true Holy Communion from the Orthodox Church into the same cauldron. At that moment, the water cooled, and the portion neither dissolved nor became wet.

[25]

The Victory of Christ

A sorcerer, aided by demonic powers, performed deceptive miracles to lure Christians away from the truth. One of his demonstrations involved entering fire and remaining unharmed, while a demon extinguished the flames.

Hearing of this, the local bishop brought the Holy Tabernacle containing the Body of Christ and approached the fire. He challenged the sorcerer to be bound and thrown into the flames, so all could see whether he would survive.

Confident in past success, the sorcerer agreed. But as soon as he was thrown into the fire, he cried out in agony:

"Help me, demon, for the fire is consuming me!"

A terrible voice responded: "I have helped you many times before, but now I cannot—for One stronger than I stands beside you."

The sorcerer was consumed by the flames and reduced to ashes.

[1]

Forty Liturgies For Health

A nobleman from Nicomedia fell gravely ill. Sensing that death was near, he summoned his wife to express his final wishes:

"Distribute my wealth to the poor and to orphans. Free the slaves. But do not give money to the priests to offer liturgies."

In his distress, however, he fervently invoked the intercession of Abba Isaiah, a holy monk who lived in asceticism near Nicomedia. Miraculously—O the wonder!—he was immediately healed.

Overjoyed, he ran to thank the elder, who glorified God for the miracle.

"My child," the elder asked, "do you recall the hour when you recovered?"

"At the exact moment I called upon your prayer," the nobleman replied.

The saint, enlightened by the Holy Spirit, then asked:

"Did you leave anything with the priests to offer liturgies for your soul's salvation?"

"No, Elder. What benefit would that bring? Wouldn't it be wasted?"

"Do not speak so. The Lord's brother, James, writes: 'Is anyone among you sick? Let him call the elders of the

Church… and the prayer of faith will save the sick.' So you see, priests' prayers are effective when offered in faith. Now, offer a gift for the liturgies, and God will show you why."

He obeyed and requested forty Divine Liturgies to be celebrated.

On the final day, after the last liturgy, he awoke and saw his house doors open and forty radiant horsemen entering—twenty on his right, twenty on his left.

"Who are you?" he asked, in awe.

"We are the forty liturgies offered on your behalf. The merciful God sent us to accompany you to His holy church. There, through the hands of the priests, Christ will unite Himself with you."

From that day on, the nobleman gave generously to fund Divine Liturgies "for the forgiveness of sins." He testified that liturgies and good deeds lift the soul from the depths to the heights of heaven.

[46]

Help for the Helpless

The extent to which the Divine Liturgy can help Christians who are commemorated in it is evident from the following incidents recounted by Saint Gregory the Dialogist, Pope of Rome (590–604):

Incident 1: A man was once held captive far from his family, bound with heavy chains. His wife regularly arranged for the Divine Liturgy to be celebrated on specific days for his sake. After years, the captive returned to his homeland. He then told his wife that on certain days, his chains would mysteriously and inexplicably loosen, giving him some relief.

Astonished, she realized that this happened precisely on the days when the Divine Liturgy was offered for his salvation.

Incident 2: Another incident involved a sailor traveling with Bishop Agathon of Panormus to Rome. During the journey, the sailor was in a small boat tied to the back of the ship. At one point, due to a storm, the rope broke, and the boat disappeared. The ship drifted to an island called Ostiva, where the bishop waited for three days in case the boat and sailor reappeared. Finally, he concluded that the sailor had drowned and ordered a Divine Liturgy to be celebrated for the repose of his soul.

When the bishop later arrived in Italy, in the city of Portus, he unexpectedly met the sailor. His joy was indescribable.

"How did you survive the shipwreck?" he asked with loving curiosity.

"For a long time, holy master," replied the sailor, "I struggled against wild waves. The boat filled with water and overturned many times. Exhausted from trying to hold on to it, I eventually fainted. Then, while I was neither awake nor asleep, someone appeared before me in the sea and offered me bread. I ate and regained strength. Shortly after, a passing ship rescued me and brought me safely to shore."

"Do you remember which day that unknown person appeared and gave you bread?" asked the bishop.

The sailor's answer amazed him—it was the same day when he had celebrated the Divine Liturgy for him on Ostiva!

[16]

St. John the Merciful, Patriarch of Alexandria (13th century fresco)
Theotokos Church, Monastery Studenica, Serbia

Respite for the Prisoner

A similar incident to the previous ones was once recounted by St. John the Merciful, Patriarch of Alexandria (610-619), to his clergy to demonstrate how beneficial liturgies are:

A young man from Cyprus, a compatriot of the saint, was taken captive to Persia and imprisoned in a place called Lethe. There was a strict Persian law that those imprisoned there would never leave alive.

However, some prisoners once managed to escape. They mistakenly informed the young man's relatives that he had died in prison. After this, his parents would bring offerings to the church three times a year for the repose of his soul, believing he was dead.

Four years passed. One day, the young man managed to escape and return to his homeland. His parents' surprise and joy were indescribable, as they welcomed him not as an escapee from prison, but as one risen from the dead.

They then told him how, for the repose of his soul, they had especially commemorated his name during the liturgies of Theophany, Pascha, and Pentecost. The young man then emotionally assured them that on those days, a radiant figure would appear and free him from his chains for a short while.

[16]

Marvelous Signs

Saint Theodore of Sykeon (6th-7th century) was born in the village of Sykeon in Anastasiopolis, the largest province of Ancyra. He was the illegitimate son of a prostitute, but this did not prevent God from making him a chosen vessel and an honorable bishop.

Theodore was born to Maria, a prostitute, and Cosmas, a messenger of Emperor Justinian. When Theodore was six years old, his mother decided to make him a soldier of the Roman Empire. However, the night before his departure, Saint George appeared to his mother in a dream and told her that Christ had other, more glorious plans for the boy.

From a young age, Theodore was drawn to a spiritual life. He spent four years reading the Holy Scriptures and praying in the church of Saint George. At fourteen, he approached a spiritual father named Glycerius, who recognized his virtue and helped him become a monk. Theodore then returned to the mountain church of Saint George the Trophy-bearer, where he dug a crypt near the Holy Altar and lived in prayer and fasting.

Eventually, Theodore became the Bishop of Anastasiopolis, but his love for the quiet monastic life led him to resign from his episcopal duties. He called together the notables of the city and all the clergy and told them that he could no longer bear the burden of being their bishop. Despite their tears and pleas for him to stay, Theodore had made his irrevocable decision. He returned to his monastery in Sykeon where he continued his ascetic life filled with miracles.

Once, a prisoner named George was brought to Theodore's cell by guards seeking his blessing. The soldiers asked the saint to counsel George. Theodore indeed admonished him, and George, deeply moved, asked to receive Holy Communion.

"Untie him from his bonds so I can give him communion, my children," the saint asked the guards.

"We dare not, Elder, because he is strong. And if he decides to do something rash, we won't be able to stop him," they explained.

Saint Theodore of Sykeon (6th-7th century)

Then the God-bearing Theodore took the Holy Chalice in his hands, raised his eyes upward and sighed. At that moment, the chains were loosened and fell to the ground with a noise.

The soldiers were frightened and ran to secure the doors.

"Don't be afraid of him," the saint reassured them. "I know his prudence. He won't do anything reckless."

Thus, Theodore gave communion to the prisoner, and afterward invited everyone to eat. After the meal, the guards put the chains back on George and continued on their way.

Saint Theodore performed many miracles during his life, including healing the sick and casting out unclean spirits. He reposed peacefully at his monastery, having lived a life devoted to Christ.

[56]

Victory Over the Demons

The desert is not only a refuge for peace-loving monks, but also a place of exile for demons, who set the most fearsome traps for the warriors of Christ.

The location of Melana was where Saint Athanasius the Athonite (10th century) practiced asceticism. The devil fought methodically to drive him away from there but failed. Thus, the saint began preparations for building the monastic complex of the Great Lavra.

However, when construction began, whatever the builders constructed during the day was torn down by demons at night.

At that point, the Holy Theotokos appeared to Saint Athanasius and said to him:

"For the work to proceed, you must build a small chapel in one day and have a Divine Liturgy performed there on the same day."

Indeed, within one day, a small church dedicated to the Holy Unmercenaries Cosmas and Damian was built and consecrated. It was so small it could barely fit the priest in the sanctuary and four or five people in the rest of the space.

Thus, through the grace of the Divine Liturgy, the demons departed, and the construction of the Lavra continued.

[31]

The Punishment of the Turk

Saint Arsenius of Cappadocia (1840-1924) was a new saintly figure from Farasa in Cappadocia, known in his homeland by the nickname "Hadjiephentis".

The people of Farasa recount many miraculous events related to the saint.

Once in Farasa, on the day of the Resurrection, a Turkish bandit chief entered the church while Saint Arsenius was celebrating the Divine Liturgy. As soon as he saw the armed and shameless Turk inside the church, the saint warned him to leave immediately. However, the Turk was undeterred. The saint calmly continued the Divine Liturgy.

When he came out for the Great Entrance, the Turk saw him not walking on the ground, but moving through the air. Seeing this miracle, he began to tremble. He tried to leave, but could not, as he felt tied by an invisible rope.

After entering the sanctuary with the Holy Gifts, the saint motioned for the Turk to leave. At that moment, the bandit chief felt released. Trembling all over, he went outside and fell down as if dead.

When the liturgy ended, the celebrant came out of the church, approached the Turk, lifted him up, and thus he was able to stand on his feet. Then he gave him a stern warning, handed him five piastres, and let him go, healthy but terrified.

[38]

The Value of the Proskomidi

The divine grace, which flows from the bloodless sacrifice, is offered not only to the living but also to the dead. This is why the celebrants continually pray not only "for health" but also "for the repose of the souls of the departed servants of God."

The greater the faith and love of the priests, the longer the list of names they commemorate during the Proskomidi.[4]

Father Savvas the spiritual father, a saintly figure from Mount Athos (1821-1908), appeared to be an insignificant monk with his tiny body. However, when he celebrated the liturgy, he looked majestic, and his face shone like that of an angel.

During the Proskomidi, he commemorated names "without number." He used a considerably large diskos,

4 The Proskomidi is the service performed at the Prothesis (a space within the sanctuary, to the left of the Holy Altar) before the Divine Liturgy. During this service, the celebrant prepares the bread and wine offered by the faithful for the celebration of the Holy Eucharist. These Gifts will later be transferred (during the Great Entrance) to the Holy Altar for their sanctification and transformation into the Body and Blood of Christ.

and for two to three hours, he would take out particles and commemorate names incessantly.

"Holy spiritual father, you tire yourself with so many names," some fathers would tell him out of love.

"I don't get tired," he would reply. "On the contrary, I feel great joy. Those commemorated benefit greatly. Their benefit is my joy."

When Father Savvas was still a young priest, he received a revelation in which God showed him the great benefit that souls derive from commemoration. He recorded this shortly before his repose, as an answer to those who asked him why he commemorated so many names daily.

"In 1843, I was given a list of names to perform a forty-day cycle of liturgies [*Sarantaliturgo*]. On the day on which I was to celebrate the final liturgy, while waiting for my elder so that I could do the preparatory prayers,[5] I fell asleep leaning on the lectern and saw the following revelatory dream:

I was dressed in priestly vestments and standing before the Holy Altar, upon which was the Holy Diskos of the liturgy, filled with the Blood of Christ.

I then saw an angel of the Lord, appearing in the form of a priest, take the paper with the names from the Proskomidi and approach the Holy Altar. There, he placed the paper near the Holy Diskos, dipped the spoon into the Blood of Christ, and began erasing one name after another until all the names were erased, and the paper was cleansed.

5 The preparatory prayers [*kairos*] are a brief service performed before the Divine Liturgy, in front of the Royal Doors, by the priests and deacons who are about to serve. It begins with a bow to the presiding hierarch or at the episcopal throne and concludes with a deep bow toward the people. If a bishop is to serve, the priests and deacons, instead of this service, simply receive the bishop's blessing and enter the sanctuary. In that case, the bishop alone performs the Kairos.

After the Divine Liturgy, I recounted this dream to my elder. He told me:

'You are not worthy for their sins to be forgiven because you commemorated them. It is through their faith that they received forgiveness for their sins.'

This dream is why I commemorate everyone's names."

[58]

Forty Liturgies "For the Repose"

Elder Daniel the Athonite (fl. 1929), a wise hesychast from Katounakia, recorded the following incident in his manuscripts, which occurred in 1869 in his hometown of Smyrna:

A virtuous Christian, nearing the end of his life, summoned his spiritual father, Fr. Dimitrios, and asked:

"I am dying today. Please tell me what I should do at this critical hour."

The priest, aware of the man's virtue and sacramental preparation, suggested:

"Give instructions to have a regular forty-day cycle of liturgies [Sarantaliturgo] performed for you at a countryside chapel after your death."

The man, named Dimitrios, accepted the suggestion and instructed his son to arrange the forty liturgies after his repose. The son promptly entrusted Fr. Dimitrios with carrying out his father's final wish.

The humble priest agreed and secluded himself for the duration of the forty days at the chapel of the Holy Apostles to perform the liturgies. Thirty-nine liturgies were completed without interruption. However, the final liturgy was scheduled for Sunday.

Saint Daniel of Katounakia

On Saturday evening, Fr. Dimitrios suffered severe tooth pain and had to return home. His wife suggested extracting the tooth, but he refused because he needed to celebrate the last liturgy the next day. By midnight, the pain worsened, forcing him to extract the tooth. Due to subsequent bleeding, he postponed the final liturgy until Monday.

Meanwhile, on Saturday afternoon, George, the son of the blessed Demetrius, prepared some money for the priest's effort, intending to give it to him the next day.

At midnight, he woke up to pray. He sat up in bed and began to recall his father's virtues, gifts, and wise words. At one point, the following thought crossed his mind: "Do the forty liturgies really benefit the souls of the departed, or did the Church establish them to comfort the living?"

Just then, he fell into a light sleep and dreamed he was in a plain of indescribable beauty. He felt unworthy to be in such a sacred and paradisiacal place. Before him stretched an endless and lush garden, fragrant with an ineffable aroma.

"This must surely be paradise!" he mused. "Oh, what bliss awaits those who live virtuously on earth!"

Examining the otherworldly beauty in amazement, he saw a brilliant palace of exquisite architectural grace, its walls gleaming with diamonds and gold. Its beauty was indescribable.

As he approached closer—what joy!—he saw his father at the palace door, radiant and splendidly dressed.

"How did you get here, my child?" he asked with gentleness and affection.

"I don't know either, father. I understand I'm not worthy of this place. But tell me, how are you faring here? How did you come? Whose palace is this?"

"The compassion of Christ the Savior, through the intercessions of the Theotokos, to whom I had particular devotion, deemed me worthy to be assigned to this place. I was actually supposed to enter the palace today. However, the builder who is constructing it experienced a hardship — he had a tooth extracted tonight — so the forty days of its construction were not completed. For this reason, I will enter tomorrow."

Afterward, George woke up in tears and amazement, but also with questions. He spent the rest of the night offering praises and glorifications to God. In the morning, after the Divine Liturgy, he took prosphora, nama wine, and pure candles and set off for the chapel of the Holy Apostles. Father Demetrios welcomed him joyfully:

"I just finished the Divine Liturgy. Thus, the forty liturgies are completed."

He said this so as not to sadden him. The visitor then recounted his night vision. When he reached the point where his father did not enter the palace because the builder had extracted his tooth, Father Demetrios felt both awe and amazement.

"I am, my dear, the builder who worked on the construction of the palace," he said with joy. "I didn't celebrate the liturgy today because I had my tooth extracted. But I will celebrate on Monday, and thus I will complete your father's spiritual palace."

[59]

The Invincible Power

The late Metropolitan of Argolida Chrysostom Deligiannopoulos (+1985) served as a military priest in Albania during the Greco-Italian war of 1940. The following testimonies are from his personal diary and oral accounts. They demonstrate that Holy Communion was

Metropolitan of Argolida, Chrysostom Deligiannopoulos

a great power that fortified the Greek fighters at the front.

March 9, 1941. Sunday. Sunday of Orthodoxy and the feast of the Forty Martyrs.

On the Albanian front, Mussolini himself is present and personally directing the famous spring offensive.

I feel a spiritual exultation, combined with intense nervousness. While we were preparing early in the morning to celebrate the Divine Liturgy in the house where we were staying, suddenly a barrage of fire from enemy mortars began.

"Father, how can we have liturgy today?" the commander asks me.

"Today it is especially imperative that we celebrate the liturgy," I replied, "so that we may come under God's protection."

The commander finally relented, and so we enjoyed the Divine Mystery with a beautiful choir of soldiers, while the surrounding area had turned into a hell of fire.

During this liturgy, we experienced the wondrous presence of Christ: Twice during its course, artillery shells grazed the edge of our house's wall, fell in the opposite space, and sank into the ground without exploding. Had they exploded, we would all have been killed inside the house… On this day, the deputy commander, the adjutant, and many soldiers of the regiment received Holy Communion.

However, as we finished the liturgy, a sad event came to give us a good lesson. Some soldiers, instead of coming to attend the liturgy, preferred to take shelter in an underground trench. And while the area was being furrowed by shells, one of them fell into the trench, killing four men and wounding three others. One was even found decapitated…

On Sunday, March 30, 1941, I started very early for the first battalion, where I celebrated the liturgy and preached. About five hundred men received Holy Communion. My hand became cramped and hurt terribly from continuously distributing the Holy Communion.

Another time, I was forced to celebrate the liturgy kneeling in a tent because it was raining continuously outside. The soldiers attended the Divine Liturgy in the rain, and at the end, they received the Immaculate Mysteries. What a moving sight! In the wild mountains, and in the rain, the soldiers came forward to unite with Christ the Savior.

[57]

The Divine Liturgy and the Figs

When Father Benedict Petrakis (+1961) was a preacher in Ioannina, he went one Sunday morning to officiate and preach at a church in the city.

Outside the church, he saw a man selling figs from his cart.

"Cover it, blessed one," he says to him, "and come inside the church to attend the liturgy. After the service, you'll sell them all."

"My dear priest," replied the man with a bold expression, "you mind your business, and I'll mind mine!"

"Well, alright… Then know that, until the liturgy ends, they will all be worm-infested," the elder says prophetically.

And indeed, they all became worm-infested, and he threw them away!

When Father Benedict was leaving the church after the liturgy, the man ran to him repentantly and asked for forgiveness. [33]

The Drunkard Priest

The bishop who told this story is still alive. It's a true story with a profound meaning, as it refers to the prayers of the living for the deceased. These prayers are always heard, but especially during the Divine Liturgy.

The bishop we mentioned had a priest in his region, Papa-Yannis, who was devout and beloved by all. He would take a bit longer during the preparation of the Holy Gifts because he read many names.

However, he had a terrible flaw: he liked wine. As good as he was at his duties, he was equally weak when it came to drinking. Many told him to cut this passion, so unbecoming of a servant of God. He understood it himself, cried with regret, made some attempts, but in a few days would start again.

One day, having again succumbed to his passion, he went to church and, half-intoxicated, began the Divine Liturgy. God allowed that at some point he stumbled inside the sanctuary, causing the Holy Gifts to fall from his hands.

He froze in fear. He fell down crying and began to gather the Body and Blood of Christ with his tongue. Not only that, but he felt guilt choking him, as it happened because he was dizzy from the wine.

He went to the bishop and confessed his terrible sin. The next day, after much consideration, the bishop sat at his desk and took his pen. He had to start the process for Papa-Yannis's defrocking, but…

As the bishop's hand hesitated to finalize the order for defrocking, he suddenly witnessed a dramatic vision. Thousands emerged from the room's walls. Their eyes were filled with sorrow, and they passed before him, shouting:

"Do not punish the priest, Your Grace! Do not defrock him! Forgive him!"

Countless multitudes—men, women, children, both well-dressed and poorly dressed—formed a true assembly of souls. All gestured toward him, pleading insistently:

"Do not do this, Your Eminence! Do not remove our priest! He remembers us and helps us in every liturgy. He truly cares for us; he is our friend! Do not defrock him! Please, no!"

The vision lasted quite a while. The bishop watched in astonishment as this sea of humanity begged and pleaded for the drunk priest. He realized that these were the souls of the deceased whom Papa-Yannis had commemorated during his liturgies. This commemoration greatly comforted them, as refreshing as water to the thirsty on a hot summer day.

"This is tangible proof," he thought, "that our prayers bring rest to the souls of the departed." Then he sent for the priest to summon him.

"Tell me, Papa-Yannis, do you commemorate many names during the preparation of the Holy Gifts when you serve the liturgy?"

"Hundreds, Your Eminence. I haven't counted them."

"Why do you do this and delay the liturgy?" the bishop pretended to scold him.

"I feel deeply sorry for the deceased because they have no help from anywhere else, except from the prayers of the Church. That's why I ask Christ to give them rest. I have a book where I write down all the names given to me for commemoration. I inherited this practice from my father, who was also a priest."

"You do well," the bishop agreed, "the souls are in need. Continue to keep this practice. Just be careful not to get drunk again. From today, you will not put wine in your mouth. This is the penance I give you. You are forgiven."

Indeed, Papa-Yannis was definitively freed from his passion for drinking. Only now he spends even more time at the preparation, commemorating the names of the "deceased."

[34]

Ὁ μελισμός (The Dividing), 14th century fresco
from Saint Andrew Church, Matka Gorge, North Macedonia

PART II

BODY AND BLOOD OF CHRIST

The suffering Christ venerated during Holy Week

The Deluded Hermit

A certain hermit, more out of ignorance than anything else, refused to accept that the Holy Bread we receive in communion is the Body of the Lord. When the elders of the Skete learned of this, they called him and instructed him in the correct teaching of the Church regarding the Immaculate Mysteries. However, he persisted in his error. The fathers left him but prayed for God to enlighten him so that he might understand the truth.

One Sunday, the hermit participated in the Divine Liturgy from the sanctuary of the Skete's church. The moment the priest took prosphora in his hands to offer it, the deluded monk was astonished to see an infant lying on the Holy Altar. And when the priest began to divide the Bread, a holy angel appeared above the Altar, holding a knife in his hand. Simultaneously with the priest, the angel also divided the divine Infant and poured His Blood into the Holy Chalice.

The hermit was disturbed. But after a while, when he went to receive communion, something even more terrifying occurred. He saw human flesh stained with blood inside the Holy Chalice. Weeping, he then confessed his error and begged the Lord to cover the Divine Mysteries with His grace so that he might dare to receive communion. Indeed, in the Holy Chalice he again saw bread and wine, from which he partook, giving thanks to God.

[55]

The Skeptical Monk

A monk was struggling with thoughts of doubt about whether the Holy Gifts are truly the Body and Blood of Christ, or merely symbols and representations. When the other monks learned of this, they invited him to a Divine Liturgy, during which they all prayed fervently for God to reveal the truth to him through a miracle, so as to dispel his doubts.

After the service, the monk shared the following with the others:

"When the deacon ascended the pulpit to read the Gospel, I saw the roof of the church open. After the prayer of Preparation [Proskomidi], I saw the heavens split apart and fire descend upon the Holy Gifts. Then a multitude of angels appeared, and among them was a Child. Along with them descended two other figures of indescribable beauty. The angels then stood in a circle around the Holy Altar, while the Child was enthroned upon it.

"When the priests approached to divide the bread of the Prothesis (Preparation), I saw two figures take the Child by His hands and feet. With a knife, they slaughtered Him, pouring His Blood into the Holy Chalice. Then they cut His Body into small portions and placed them on the pieces of bread. Immediately, the bread itself was transformed into flesh.

"During the communion hymn 'With fear of God…,' the brothers who approached were offered pieces of flesh. But as soon as they said, 'Amen,' it became bread in their hands.[6]

"When I approached, I was given flesh and could not partake. Then I heard a voice whisper in my ear: 'Why do you not commune? Is this not precisely what you asked

6 See footnote 1.

for?' 'Have mercy on me, Lord. I cannot consume flesh.' 'Learn then: if humans could partake of pure flesh, the Holy Chalice would contain flesh as you saw. But since they cannot, God ordained the bread of the Prothesis. If you believe this consecrated Bread is Christ's very Body, receive what you hold in your hand!'

"'I believe, Lord,' I answered, broken-hearted. At once, the flesh I held became bread again. I gave thanks to God and communed.

"After the sacred mysteries concluded, I saw the church roof open once more and the angelic hosts ascend back to heaven."

[16, 52]

A Portion of God's Own Flesh

A stylite (pillar-dwelling ascetic) near Damascus once became scandalized upon learning that a local priest had fallen into carnal sin. When the priest later came to celebrate liturgy at the monastery where the stylite resided, the ascetic lowered a basket to receive the Holy Communion. However, he hesitated to partake, doubting: "Has this portion been sanctified? Did the Holy Spirit descend upon it, or was it hindered by the priest's sin? Should I, scandalized by this priest, receive it or not?"

As the priest divided the Holy Body during the liturgy, a portion fell onto the Altar and transformed into fresh, bleeding flesh before the eyes of all present. When the priest touched it, the flesh adhered to his finger like living meat. As he pulled back, three drops of blood fell onto the Altar's marble, staining the liturgical coverings.

Saint Anastasius of Sinai
(14th century icon)
Monastery of St. Catherine,
Sinai, Egypt

Upon witnessing this miracle, the stylite communed with fear and trembling, confessing his doubt to all.

Saint Anastasios of Sinai, who narrated this miraculous story, was an eyewitness to the event. He was honored to see, venerate, and take with him a piece of the divine-flesh portion [*theósarki merída*].

At one point, while in Jerusalem, he encountered a demon-possessed individual. With unwavering faith, he hung the holy portion around the afflicted person's neck in a small pouch. Within a few days, the individual was completely healed.

[2]

The Appearance of the Theotokos

A very virtuous priest named Pelagius lived in the land of the Alemanni[7] and had a special devotion to the Most Holy Theotokos. However, the devil envied him and planted thoughts of doubt in his mind about the Holy Communion.

7 The Alemanni were a Germanic tribe that emerged in the 2nd century. They succeeded in establishing the Duchy of Alamannia in the 10th century, which, however, was dissolved in the 11th century.

"How is it possible," he wondered, "for bread to become the Body and wine to become the Blood of Christ?"

These thoughts caused him great sorrow, but he did not dare to seek advice from anyone. Instead, he turned directly to the Virgin Mary and prayed fervently for her to enlighten him on this matter.

One day, while celebrating the Divine Liturgy, as he reached the hymn "Especially for our Most Holy, Pure Lady...," the Holy Bread disappeared from the paten. Frightened, Pelagius searched everywhere but could not find it.

"Mother of God!" he cried out in terror. "I know that because of my lack of faith and doubt, Christ has rejected me and departed so that I, unworthy as I am, may not partake. But you, please intercede with Him to forgive me!"

He then saw before the Holy Altar the Most Glorious Queen holding the divine Infant in her arms, saying to him: "This Child is the Creator of the universe, the Son, and Word of God; perfect God and perfect man. He died on the Cross for the salvation of the world and rose again. Even now, He descends daily in a wondrous manner into the form of bread and wine, out of His great love for humanity, and offers Himself to them for the sanctification of their souls. Touch Him and examine Him fearlessly to confirm that this is a true vision—that He is a real body with flesh and blood, as I bore Him. This is precisely how bread and wine become during your liturgy. However, since human nature cannot consume raw flesh or drink blood, in His infinite wisdom, the Almighty offers Himself in the form of bread and wine so that everyone may partake of Him with longing and desire. Commune with reverence and faith, for whoever receives Him worthily becomes a participant in His divine glory."

With these words, the Lady placed the Infant on the Holy Altar, worshiped Him humbly, and then disappeared.

Then the priest, with fear and joy, took the divine Infant into his hands, kissed Him reverently, and confirmed that He was indeed a living child with real flesh. He then placed Him on the Holy Altar, fell to the ground, and prayed with tears:

"I believe, Lord, and I confess that You are the Son of God, born of the ever-virgin Mary. I thank You for the grace I, unworthy as I am, have received today, and I beg You to forgive my former doubt. Now, please grant me to receive You not as an Infant but as bread."

After praying with faith, he stood up and saw before him the Holy Bread as it had been before. He communed with joy and continued for the rest of his life to celebrate the Divine Mysteries with great reverence.

[1]

The Vision of the Saracen

A certain emir[8] once sent his nephew to Diospolis in Syria for some business. In this city, the nephew encountered a magnificent church dedicated to Saint George. He immediately ordered his servants to move his belongings into the catechumen area of the church, where he also settled himself. Then he commanded that his twelve camels be brought into the church, despite the priests' protests and pleas. However, as soon as the camels entered the church, they fell dead to the ground, leaving the emir's nephew amazed at the irresistible power of Saint George.

8 Emir or amir (from the Arabic *amīr* = commander): A Muslim ruler or governor of a large province.

The next day, while the priest was celebrating the Divine Liturgy, the Saracen watched from the catechumen area. At that moment, the merciful God opened the eyes of his soul, and what did he see? He saw the priest slaughtering a small child and pouring its blood into the Holy Chalice, while cutting its body and placing it on the sacred paten.

When communion began, the Saracen observed in astonishment as the priest distributed to the people the flesh and blood of the child. After the liturgy, the priest took some of the best offerings (prosphora) and brought them as a gift to the Saracen.

"What are these?" he asked.

"These, my lord," replied the priest, "are breads offered by believers. We use them to celebrate our Church's liturgy."

"Did you use these to celebrate today?" asked the Saracen angrily. "Did I not see you slaughtering a child and giving its flesh and blood to the people? Do you think I didn't see all that, you criminal and murderer?"

The priest was terrified. He glorified God and said: "I believe, my lord, that God has placed you among those destined for salvation since He has granted you to witness such a dreadful mystery. I have never been worthy to see such a vision myself; I only ever see bread and wine before me. We believe that the bread and wine offered in our liturgy become the Body and Blood of Christ. However, this marvelous sight is not revealed to everyone."

Hearing this explanation, the Saracen was filled with wonder and decided to become a Christian. He was baptized, went to Sinai, became a monk, and later sealed his Orthodox faith with martyrdom.

[30]

The "Sin" of Elder Augustine

A blessed Athonite monk, Elder Augustine the Russian (1882–1965), was very virtuous, very humble, and a tireless spiritual struggler.

One day, the devil appeared in his cell in the form of a terrifying dog, spitting fire from its mouth, and charged at the elder to strangle him, saying that he was being tormented by the elder's prayers.

Elder Augustine grabbed him and threw him against the wall, shouting: "Evil devil, why do you attack God's creatures?"

The devil, terrified by this unexpected reaction, vanished. However, the exceedingly kind and simple elder felt remorse afterward because… he had struck the devil! He anxiously waited for dawn to go to his spiritual father and confess his "sin."

At first light, he walked to Provata (a one-and-a-half-hour distance from his cell), where his spiritual father resided, and confessed.

"My spiritual father was very understanding," Elder Augustine later recounted, "and he didn't impose any penance on me but told me to receive Holy Communion. Out of joy, I prayed the Jesus Prayer with my prayer rope all night long. Then I went to the Divine Liturgy and communed."

"When the priest placed the Holy Spoon in my mouth," he continued, "I saw Holy Communion as a piece of flesh and blood! I chewed it to swallow it! At the same time, I felt such great joy that I could hardly bear it. Sweet tears streamed from my eyes, and my head shone like a lamp. I quickly left so that the other fathers wouldn't see me, and read the thanksgiving prayers for Holy Communion alone in my cell."

[39]

Lavra of Saint Alexander Nevsky
in Saint Petersburg, Russia, as it looks today.

A Convincing Proof

In the Holy Church of the Holy Cross at the Lavra of Saint Alexander Nevsky, in Saint Petersburg, Russia, the following extraordinary event once occurred:

During a Divine Liturgy, the officiating bishop, Stephen, after reciting the prayer "I believe, O Lord, and I confess…,"[9] lifted the cover of the Holy Chalice and stood stunned. Inside, he saw human flesh and blood! Turning to the deacon, who later became Starets Samson (+1979), he asked: "Do you see this, Father?"

What could they do? The bishop placed the Holy Chalice on the Altar, knelt down, and pleaded with the

9 According to the Russian liturgical tradition, after the proclamation "With fear of God..." the celebrant recites the prayer of Holy Communion, "I believe, O Lord, and I confess...," and then proceeds to administer Communion to the faithful.

Lord for mercy. How could he distribute human flesh to the faithful? Who would dare to receive it?

After praying for a quarter of an hour with his hands raised, he looked again into the Holy Chalice. The flesh and blood had transformed back into bread and wine. He then went out and communed the faithful.

The clergy who learned of this miracle said that God allowed it to strengthen their faith. Deacon Samson, who held the Holy Chalice, confessed that this event gave him extraordinary strength and consolation. He believed absolutely and undoubtedly that the Holy Eucharist is truly the precious Body and Blood of the Savior.

He was convinced himself, but also shared it with others so that all who heard about it would gain strength and joy. This miraculous sign, as he said, was also an occasion for clergy to acquire greater humility and recognize their unworthiness.

[50]

Blood of the Master

During the Divine Liturgy in the village of Zarqa, Jordan, on April 21, 1991, after the Great Entrance, the Orthodox priest placed the Holy Gifts on the Altar. Suddenly, he saw the paten filled with blood. Warm blood was also flowing from the Holy Bread. The priest cried out, and the faithful rushed to the sanctuary to see what was happening.

Witnessing this miraculous event, they were left speechless. Some tried to partake of a few drops of blood, while others attempted to anoint their bodies with it.

An eyewitness recounts: "I visited the city to see the divine sign up close. Thousands of people had flooded the area. The priest had managed to preserve two small pieces of Bread. I confess that what I saw was not bread and wine. It was the Body and Blood of Jesus Christ."

[6, 35]

Angels processing during the Heavenly Liturgy.

PART III

HEAVEN ON EARTH

The Transfiguration (early 15th century fresco)
by Theophanes the Greek

Light and Fire

Saint Pancratius of Taormina, originally from Antioch, lived during the apostolic era. As a young man, he visited Jerusalem with his parents, where he was baptized. After their passing, he freed their slaves, distributed his wealth to the poor, and dedicated himself to preaching the Gospel. Following instructions from the Apostle Peter, he traveled to Sicily and became the Bishop of Taormina.

Through his inspired teachings and miracles, Saint Pancratius converted many to Christianity, including the island's governor, Boniface. When Boniface heard of the saint's supernatural works, he visited him and saw him clothed in priestly garments and bathed in divine light. During a Divine Liturgy held in a room of Boniface's residence, at the "Glory to the Father…" of the Trisagion Hymn, the roof miraculously opened, and a dazzling lightning bolt descended upon Boniface and his attendants. Terrified, they all fell to the ground but afterward wholeheartedly embraced Christ.

Soon after, Sicily's first Christian church was built. When it was completed, Saint Pancratius officiated at its inaugural Divine Liturgy. Those present witnessed an extraordinary sight: a fiery and unquenchable light illuminated the entire space in a magnificent way. At the same time, something even more miraculous occurred—when the saint concluded

Saint Pancratius of Taormina

the Liturgy, all the idols in Taormina's pagan temples collapsed and shattered.

Shortly afterward, Saint Pancratius baptized 8,000 men in a single day, not counting women and children. He then celebrated Divine Liturgy for them. During the elevation of the Holy Gifts, the roof of the church opened again, and heavenly light descended upon him. The congregation was awestruck and fearful. When it came time for Communion, no one dared approach because they saw Saint Pancratius' face transformed and fiery. He reassured them: "Come forward, my children; do not be afraid. This fire does not burn but illuminates those who partake of the Body and Blood of our Lord with faith."

Encouraged by his words, the newly baptized approached to receive Communion with reverence. Those who were not yet baptized were later catechized by Saint Pancratius and baptized within a few days.

[11, 22, 54]

Heavenly Guardians

During the Divine Liturgy, Saint John Chrysostom (4th century), with his gift of spiritual insight, often saw holy angels guarding and watching over the church, especially during the bloodless sacrifice. He shared this vision with his spiritual friends, saying:

"When the priest begins to prepare the offerings, angelic forces immediately descend from heaven, dressed in radiant and wondrous garments. With bare feet and bowed faces, they surround the Holy Altar and remain there quietly and reverently until the end of the Divine Liturgy. Afterward, they disperse throughout the church, assisting the clergy in distributing the Immaculate Mysteries to the faithful and strengthening them in faith."

[5]

Burning but Not Consumed

During a Sunday Divine Liturgy, a bishop visited a village in his diocese with his entourage. There, he sought out the parish priest and asked him to celebrate the Divine Mystagogy.

The priest was a simple and uneducated villager. However, as soon as he stood before the Holy Altar, fiery flames surrounded him without burning him!

Astonished by the sight, the bishop approached him after the liturgy and said: "Bless me, worthy servant of God!"

The priest was bewildered and replied: "How is it possible for a bishop to be blessed by a priest?"

The bishop answered humbly: "I am not worthy to bless a priest who offers to God the Holy Gifts 'burning' with supernatural fire, 'yet not consumed.' As the holy apostle says, 'The lesser is blessed by the greater.'"

The priest responded with humility: "Is it ever possible," he said, "for a clergyman to celebrate the awesome mysteries without being surrounded by divine fire?"

The bishop marveled at the priest's purity of soul and unpretentious demeanor, and departed spiritually enriched.

[16]

Saint Euthymius the Great (13th century fresco)
Protato Church, Karyes, Mount Athos (Greece)

The Fiery Covering

During the life of Saint Euthymius the Great (4th century), a remarkable appearance of divine fire occurred during the Divine Liturgy. One Sunday, Saint Euthymius was celebrating the liturgy with his disciple Domitian. At one point, Terebonas, a former Saracen who was standing nearby, saw fire descending from heaven. The fire spread over the Altar like a large white cloth and covered both Saint Euthymius and Domitian. Witnessing this extraordinary miracle, Terebonas was filled with fear and stepped back. The divine fire remained from the beginning to the end of the Trisagion Hymn.

Apart from Saint Euthymius and Domitian, another witness of this miracle was Monk Gavriilios, who had been living in the monastery for twenty-five years and was known for his spiritual purity.

Saint Euthymius often experienced such divine phenomena. Many times, while celebrating the liturgy, he saw holy angels serving alongside him. Additionally, when distributing Holy Communion to the monks, he would see some illuminated by divine light while others were condemned as unworthy of this divine illumination. For this reason, he always advised careful preparation, self-examination, and repentance before approaching the mystery of the Holy Eucharist.

[48]

Angel Concelebrants

During a Divine Liturgy, Saint Nephon, Bishop of Constantiana (4th century), was granted the vision of numerous divine phenomena through the enlightened eyes of his soul.

As the priest proclaimed, "Blessed is the Kingdom...," Saint Nephon saw fire descending from heaven and enveloping the Holy Altar and the priest, though the priest himself was unaware. Later, during the chanting of the Trisagion Hymn by the congregation, four angels descended and joined in singing.

During the reading of the Epistle, Saint Paul appeared and guided the reader. Following this, at the "Alleluia" after the Epistle, the voices of the people ascended to heaven as a fiery, tightly woven rope. During the Gospel reading, each word emerged like a flame from the priest's mouth and rose to the heavens.

Just before the entrance of the Holy Gifts, Saint Nephon suddenly saw heaven open and an indescribable, otherworldly fragrance pour forth. Angels descended from above, singing hymns and praises to Christ, the Lamb, and Son of God. Then, a pure and exceedingly graceful Infant appeared, carried by angels who placed Him on the Holy Paten where the Holy Gifts were prepared. Around Him gathered a multitude of radiant young men dressed in white, gazing with awe and reverence at His divine beauty.

When it was time for the Great Entrance, the priest approached to take up the Holy Paten and Chalice. He lifted them onto his head along with the Infant. As they exited with "The Holy Things are for the holy," while the congregation sang devoutly, Saint Nephon saw angels fluttering around the priest. Two Cherubim and two Seraphim walked ahead of him, accompanied by countless other angels singing indescribable hymns with joy.

When the priest reached the Holy Altar and placed down the Holy Gifts, angels covered them with their wings.

Saint Nephon, Bishop of Constantiana (14th century fresco),
Monastery Gračanica, Serbia

The two Cherubim stood to his right and two Seraphim to his left, though he could not see them.

The Divine Mystagogy continued. After chanting "I believe…," they reached the consecration of the Holy Gifts. The priest blessed them and said: "…transforming them by Your Holy Spirit. Amen; Amen; Amen." At that moment, Saint Nephon saw an angel take a knife and slaughter the Infant. The angel poured His blood into the Holy Chalice, while His body was divided and placed on the paten. The angel then returned solemnly to his place.

During the Divine Liturgy, as the priest elevated the Holy Bread and proclaimed "The Holy Things are for the holy," while the congregation chanted "One is holy, one is Lord, Jesus Christ…," a member of the congregation turned to Saint Nephon and asked quietly: "Why does the priest say 'The Holy Things are for the holy'?"

Saint Nephon replied: "He says it for all of us, my child. It means: Let those who are holy approach the holy members of Christ!"

The man, who was simple-minded, asked again: "And what is holiness, Father?"

Saint Nephon explained: "If you are immoral, do not dare to partake in such a great mystery. If you harbor enmity toward someone, do not approach. If you mock, curse, or judge your neighbor, stay away from Holy Communion. First examine yourself, and if you are virtuous, then approach. But if you are not, leave!"

Meanwhile, the priest proclaimed: "With fear of God, faith, and love draw near."

Saint Nephon observed those receiving Communion. Some had their faces darken as they received the Holy Mysteries, while others shone like the sun. Angels stood nearby with reverence during Communion. When a devout person communed, they placed a crown on their head.

Conversely, when a sinner approached unworthily, the angels turned their faces away in visible disgust. In such cases, the Holy Mysteries seemed to vanish from the Holy Spoon so that the sinner appeared not to receive Christ's Body and Blood within them. They left, darkened and rejected by the Lord.

After the liturgy concluded and the priest consumed the remaining Gifts (the "Katalysis"), Saint Nephon witnessed once again the Infant alive in the hands of holy angels! Suddenly, the roof of the church seemed to split in two. From there, the angels ascended with the Child to heaven with hymns and praises as they had brought Him down earlier. A sublime fragrance spread throughout once again.

[47]

Equal Sins

The city of Idades (modern-day Kition) was a commercial hub in Cyprus. Nearby was the monastery of Philoxenus.

In this monastery, during the 6th century, lived a monk named Elder Isidore, who wept incessantly with sobs. To anyone who approached him and tried to comfort him, asking him to ease his mourning, he would say: "I am very sinful. There has never been anyone as sinful as me from Adam until today. And don't think I am exaggerating. I have never found in any person a sin as grave as the one I committed."

He would then recount his story: "When I was in the world, I had a Christian wife who feared God, while I belonged to the heresy of Severus. One day, I learned that my wife had gone to receive Holy Communion at the neighboring church. I ran to stop her but found her already returning home after communing. Immediately, I grabbed her by the neck and forced her to vomit the Holy Portion, which I then took and threw out of the window into the mud. At that moment, I saw a dove descend and take up the Holy Communion."

"Two days later, a black man dressed in rags appeared before me and said: 'You and I have been condemned to the same punishment.' 'Who are you?' I asked him. 'I am the one who struck our Lord Jesus Christ on the jaw during His Passion,' he replied. And then he vanished."

"That is why," concluded the monk, "I cannot stop mourning."

[46]

"While the Doors Were Shut"

Abba Matthias, one of the holy fathers of the Sinai desert, recounted the following:

"When I was living in Arandoula, I kept the Holy Communion in the tabernacle of the church, securely locked and sealed. Every Sunday, I would distribute the Lord's Body to the captives in that desert.

"However, many times I would go to the church on Sunday and find the tabernacle open. Saddened by this, I decided to seal it with wax and a seal after first counting the holy portions.

"The following Sunday, I found the seal intact. But when I opened the cabinet, I discovered that three portions were missing.

"I began to be tormented by thoughts. Then, on another Sunday, three monks appeared to me in my sleep. After waking me, they said: 'Get up; it is time for prayer!'

"'Who are you, fathers, and where do you come from?' I asked them.

"'We,' they replied, 'are sinners who often come here to commune. From now on, do not concern yourself with this matter.'

"Then I understood that they were hermits and thanked God for granting our generation such testimonies."

[52]

By the Hand of an Angel

Saint Macarius of Alexandria (January 19), an ascetic and presbyter of the so-called "Cells" in the Egyptian desert, is remembered for his angelic life and his victories over demons, as recorded by Palladius in the Lausiac History. As a priest and celebrant, he had many wondrous experiences, one of which involved the ascetic Mark.

Saint Macarius of Alexandria (18th century fresco), Vatopedi Monastery, Mount Athos (Greece)

Saint Macarius recounted: "I observed carefully that every time I administered Holy Communion to the ascetic Mark, it was never I who offered him the Lord's Body. Instead, an angel would take it from the Holy Altar and give it to him. I could even see the angel's hand as he gave Holy Communion to the monk."

[40]

The Holy Communion that Sprouted Ears of Wheat

In the city of Seleucia in Syria, during the episcopacy of Dionysius (6th century), there lived a very wealthy and devout merchant. However, he was a heretic and adhered to the doctrines of Severus. This merchant had an employee who was Orthodox and followed the Holy and Apostolic Church.

According to the custom of the time,[10] the Orthodox man received Holy Communion on Holy Thursday, placed it in a small case, and locked it in a cabinet. After Easter, he left for business in Constantinople, forgetting the holy portions in the cabinet. However, he had left the key with his employer.

One day, the heretic opened the cabinet and found the box containing the holy portions. Saddened by this discovery, he did not know what to do with them since they belonged to the Orthodox Church, and he himself did not wish to partake of them. He decided to leave them in the cabinet, thinking that his employee would soon return and consume them.

A year passed. Holy Thursday came again, but the employee had not yet returned. The employer then decided to burn the portions so they would not remain for another year. He opened the cabinet, and what did he see? All the portions had sprouted ears of wheat!

Fear and trembling seized him. He immediately took them and ran to Bishop Dionysius, crying out, "Lord, have mercy!"

All the Orthodox Christians witnessed this miracle and glorified God. This event even led many people to believe and join the Holy, Catholic, and Apostolic Church.

[25]

---

10 See footnote 1.

"The Law Is Not Made for a Righteous Man"

Ten miles from the city of Aegeae in Cilicia, in the village of Mardardos, there lived an elderly Levite renowned for his virtue.

One day, however, the villagers went to complain to the Bishop of Aegeae, saying,

"Take this priest from our village, because he causes us much grief. Every Sunday he celebrates the Divine Liturgy at three o'clock in the afternoon and does not keep the established order."

Straightaway the bishop called the parish priest and said to him in private:

"Why, dear elder, do you do such a thing? Do you not know the order of our Church?"

"I know it, master, and you are right. But here is what happens: after the night-time Sunday service, I sit before the Holy Altar awaiting the descent of the Holy Spirit; and when I see the Comforter overshadowing it, then I begin the Liturgy."

The bishop marveled at the virtue of the elderly priest and informed the villagers, who left in peace giving glory to God.

[25]

The Slandered Bishop

Thirty miles from Rome was the little town of Romilla. Once, some inhabitants of Romilla brought charges against their virtuous bishop before the pope of Rome Agapetus (535-536), saying that their bishop used the Holy Chalice in his daily meals.

Dumbfounded by what he heard, the pope sent and had the bishop brought to Rome in chains and on foot. He immediately imprisoned him.

Three days passed. On Saturday night, the pope saw someone in his sleep who said to him: "This Sunday, neither you nor anyone else will celebrate the liturgy but the imprisoned bishop. He is the one I want to officiate."

Because the pope doubted, the voice was heard a second and a third time: "I told you that the imprisoned bishop will officiate!"

When the Pope awoke, he summoned the bishop and asked him: "What is your spiritual practice?"

"I am a sinner," replied the bishop.

Since he revealed nothing else, the Pope said to him: "Today you will celebrate the liturgy."

The bishop obeyed. When he stood at the Holy Altar and completed the prayer of preparation, before saying the final consecration prayer, he began the Holy Anaphora for a second, third, and fourth time.

"What is happening?" asked the Pope. "Why have you started the prayer four times without completing it?"

"Forgive me," replied the bishop, "but I did not see, as I usually do, the descent of the Holy Spirit. If you wish, remove from the Altar the deacon holding the fan because I do not dare to tell him myself."

When the deacon was removed, both the Pope and the bishop immediately saw the presence of the Holy Spirit. But something else happened as well: The veil above the Holy Altar lifted on its own and covered the Pope, the bishop, all the deacons, and the Holy Altar for three hours!

At that moment, Saint Agapetos realized that this bishop was very virtuous and had been falsely accused.

[25]

The Correction of the Irregularity

An elder, pure and holy, would see angels to his right and left every time he celebrated the liturgy. He had received the order of the liturgy from heretics, and being inexperienced in divine doctrines, he recited the prayers of the anaphora with simplicity and innocence, unaware that he was saying them incorrectly.

However, by God's providence, a brother who was well-versed in divine doctrines once visited him. This brother was a deacon and happened to be present when the elder was celebrating the liturgy. He noticed the error and said to him: "Father, what you're saying in the liturgy is not of the Orthodox faith."

But the elder, because he saw angels at that time, paid no attention to his words. The deacon persisted in pointing out the doctrinal error: "You're mistaken, old man. The Church doesn't accept these things."

Then the elder, seeing the deacon's persistence, asked the angels who stood by him during a liturgy: "What is this that the deacon is telling me?"

"He's right," they replied. "You should accept what he says."

"And why haven't you told me this for so long?" the elder asked.

"Because God ordained it this way: for a person to be corrected by other people."

From then on, the elder corrected himself, giving thanks to God and the deacon.

[25]

The Doxology of Creation

On Mount Sinai, at the Holy Summit, the Divine Liturgy of Saint James was once celebrated on the day of Pentecost. Many monks had gathered to honor the feast.

At the moment when the priest proclaimed, "The triumphant hymn of Your magnificent glory, singing with bright voice, crying out, glorifying, exclaiming and saying," a rumbling sound was heard, to which all the mountains responded with a certain echo and another fearful rumbling of "Holy, Holy, Holy, Lord of Sabaoth…"

This rumbling and echo continued for half an hour. However, not everyone heard it, but only those who had ears suitable for hearing the hymn of the angels.

[17]

Saint Theodore and the Holy Bread

On the feast day of Saint Antioch the Martyr, Saint Theodore of Sykeon (6th-7th century) was celebrating the Divine Liturgy in the church dedicated to this saint. At the moment when he proclaimed "The Holy Things for the holy," he raised the paten high, according to local custom, to elevate the Holy Bread. Then something miraculous occurred:

The Holy Bread, as if leaping with joy, rose for a long time above the paten, and then descended, striking against it. Everyone saw and heard this. In this way, the Holy Bread revealed that the sacrifice of the celebrant was acceptable to God. The faithful watched this miracle with fear and amazement, while the saint, filled with joy and tears of compunction, glorified God for His goodness.

On another occasion, the saint was celebrating the Divine Liturgy in the church of Saint George using a dry prosphora (offering bread). A faithful attendee, the patrician Photios, while observing the Holy Bread being offered, noticed that much heat was emanating from it. "The bread must be freshly baked," he thought.

However, when he approached to receive Communion, he was puzzled because the portion he received was very dry. After the dismissal, he mentioned what he had seen to the saint and asked for an explanation.

"This miracle," replied the saint, "was revealed to you, my child, because you are worthy. The grace of the Gifts contracts and ascends from us to heaven so that, due to our unworthiness and sins, we may be tested in our lives with many sorrows and dangers. Let us pray, however, to the merciful God that what He commands may be accomplished with love for mankind."

[56]

Saint Athanasia of Aegina

Saint Athanasia, whose memory is celebrated on April 18, was born and lived as an ascetic on Aegina during the years of idolatry. Because of her great virtue, she was appointed abbess of a group of nuns, who had as their caretaker and spiritual guide the presbyter Matthias, abbot of an ascetic community.

This God-loving man experienced such deep compunction when celebrating the Divine Liturgy that those who saw him derived great spiritual benefit. Matthias had a profound love for the Apostle and Evangelist John.

Saint Athanasia of Aegina

One year, on the feast day of the saint, as he was preparing to celebrate the bloodless sacrifice, he was filled with ineffable compunction. "I wonder," he asked someone beside him, "is there anyone today worthy to go to Ephesus and see the Apostle John?"

The liturgy began. And blessed Matthias, because of his faith and love for the saint, was deemed worthy to see him present at the Holy Altar from the beginning to the end of the Divine Mystagogy. And he was not the only one who saw him. Two others who were near him during the mystery also witnessed this. For three days, Matthias felt such deep compunction that he could not taste material food.

Saint Athanasia was a worthy disciple of such a spiritual teacher. She sealed her holy life with a blessed death. And when forty days had passed since her departure, the following miraculous event occurred:

While the Divine Liturgy had begun, the Lord opened the eyes of the souls of the two leading nuns in the choir, and what did they see! In the center of the church, two awe-inspiring men in radiant garments had Athanasia between them.

Immediately, they brought out a purple robe adorned with precious stones and pearls, and dressed her like a queen. Then they decorated her head with a crown that had crosses in front and back, and after giving her a staff adorned with precious stones, they led her to the Holy Altar.

At the same time, the reliquary containing the remains of the saint began to creak. And this creaking continued until a full year had passed.

[53]

Like a Flame of Fire

Saint Sergius of Radonezh (+1392) is the founder of the famous Trinity Lavra in Zagorsk, Moscow, and one of the most beloved saints of the Russian people.

Each time he celebrated the Divine Liturgy, God granted him the honor of having an angel as his co-celebrant. Once, Father Symeon, who was serving as an ecclesiarch, saw a flame

An angel stands with St. Sergius of Radonezh while fire emerges from the altar and fills the chalice. Fresco from the Trinity Lavra of St. Sergius.

emerging from the Holy Altar and surrounding the saint. He saw him completely bathed in this otherworldly light.

When the saint prepared to receive Communion, the flame rose, gathered like a veil, and plunged into the Holy Chalice. After communing, he moved away from the Holy Altar and the astonished monk asked: "Why, my child, do you appear so troubled?"

"I was deemed worthy, Elder, to see the grace of the Holy Spirit surrounding you!"

Then the saint told him emphatically: "As long as I live, do not reveal to anyone what you have seen!"

[37]

The Conversion of an Unbeliever

Among the holy martyrs of our Church is included the New Martyr Ahmed (17th century). He was a Turk from Constantinople.

In his house, he had two Russian captive women as servants, one young and one elderly. Both were devout. The older woman used to go to church on every feast day. There she would receive antidoron (blessed bread) and holy water, and would bring some to the young woman. But every time this happened, Ahmed noticed a wonderful fragrance coming from the girl's mouth.

"What is it that you eat that makes your mouth so fragrant?" he asked her.

"Nothing special," she replied.

"That can't be. Something is happening," the Turk insisted.

"Here's what happens," the young woman explained. "I eat blessed bread that the old woman brings me from the Christian church."

Saint Ahmed the Calligrapher

Then Ahmed, out of curiosity, wanted to see how Christians worship in their churches. So he dressed as a Christian and went to the Patriarchal Church, where he attended the Divine Liturgy.

During the service, Christ the Lord permitted a second miracle:

When the priest was walking toward the Royal Doors, Ahmed saw him elevated in the air and radiant with light. Luminous rays fell from his body and illuminated the heads of the Christians. However, they did not illuminate Ahmed's head.

The man of another faith was deeply moved by what he saw. The eyes of his soul opened, and he believed without hesitation in the true God. He asked the priest to baptize him. Later, on May 3, 1682, he confessed his faith in an assembly of nobles, whereupon he was deemed worthy to receive the baptism of martyrdom.

[22]

The Radiant Celebrant

The New Martyr Saint James of Mount Athos (November 1) once recounted to his disciple Marcian the wondrous things he saw during a Divine Liturgy:

"As the priest was putting on his priestly vestments, the light of angels shone before him, like the sun shining at dawn before it rises. When he began the Proskomidi (Preparation of the Gifts), four angelic orders came and stood at the four corners of the church."

"When he finished the Proskomidi, he covered the precious Gifts with the sacred veils, which were simultaneously enveloped in radiance. At the time of the Great Entrance, when the Holy Gifts were brought out, a light preceded them, covering the people. The same light later encircled the Holy Altar when the Chalice was placed upon it. Outside this luminous circle, the angels stood reverently, not daring to approach."

"The light did not leave the priest throughout the entire liturgy. An invisible flame came from his mouth when he pronounced the prayers and read the Gospel. Also, when he raised his hands, light poured from his fingers."

"After the consecration, I saw the Lord as an infant seated on the paten amidst radiant glory. The priest divided Him into four parts, and His precious Blood was poured into the Holy Chalice, from which the celebrant communed."

"When the Mystagogy was finished, I again saw the divine Infant, whole and entire, ascending to heaven with glory and honor, accompanied by the holy angels."

[5]

The Lord in Glory

Saint Seraphim of Sarov (1759-1833), this beloved saint of the Orthodox, was strengthened in his spiritual struggles by divine providence through spiritual visions that

Holy New Martyr James of Mount Athos
and his two disciples James the Deacon and Dionysius the Monk

comforted his soul. As a deacon, he occasionally saw during services holy angels singing and serving alongside the monks.

"Once," he recounts, "I was celebrating the liturgy on Holy Thursday. After the Small Entrance and the readings, I, humble as I am, proclaimed beside the Holy Altar: 'Lord, save the pious and hear us.' Then I went to the Beautiful Gate and, raising the orarion toward the congregation, completed the prayer of the Trisagion Hymn: 'And unto the ages of ages.'

"At that moment, a light shone before me. Looking in that direction, I saw our Lord Jesus Christ, in the form of the Son of Man, shining more brilliantly than the sun in abundant light. He was surrounded, like a swarm of bees, by the heavenly powers of angels, archangels, cherubim, and seraphim.

"He had entered through the western door and, walking on air, stood opposite the ambo. Raising His hand, He blessed the celebrants and those praying. Finally, He entered the place where His icon is located, next to the Beautiful Gate. My heart leaped with joy, with the sweetest love for the Lord."

It is noteworthy that this vision occurred during the entrance of the priests into the sanctuary, which symbolizes their entrance into heaven itself. "Grant, O Lord," the priest prays quietly at that moment, "that with our entrance there may be an entrance of holy angels, concelebrating with us and glorifying Your goodness." Moreover, after the entrance, the angelic hymn is chanted: "Holy God, Holy Mighty, Holy Immortal, have mercy on us."

This vision reveals that the heavenly powers invisibly concelebrate with us. Therefore, let every believer know that they pray among angels, as if they were in heaven.

[36]

The Strange Liturgist

The Starets Theophilus, hieromonk (1788-1853, Russian), a runaway who practiced in various monasteries and hermitages of Kiev, never ceased, even when celebrating the liturgy, to scandalize the other brothers with his strange behavior.

The then Metropolitan of Kiev, Filaret, annoyed by all this, called his advisors to examine with them the case of the hieromonk. Soon, however, light was shed on the matter by a brother, to whom the starets had given explanations for his "inappropriate" behavior during the sacred services:

"God," he had told him confidentially, "sees my simplicity. I celebrate the liturgy according to the proper order, read all the required prayers, and honor the presiding celebrant as my superior. However, as I immerse myself in the contemplation of the mystery being performed, I forget myself and everything around me.

"During the Divine Liturgy, I see a cross-shaped ray descending from above and hovering over the celebrants.

"I also see a kind of dew descending upon the precious Gifts, and radiant angels flying above the Holy Altar singing: 'Holy, Holy, Holy, Lord of Sabaoth; heaven and earth are full of Your glory.' Then my whole being is ineffably enraptured, and it is impossible for me to draw my attention away from this most delightful vision.

"Brother, I am not giving you excuses, but the pure truth. I ask you, however, not to reveal what I have told you, so that others may not be scandalized by me, the filthy sinner."

[2]

The Holy Altar in Flames

In the past century in Asia Minor lived a holy but obscure priest, Father John. He was married with a family, from Gelveri in Cappadocia. On weekdays, he worked in the fields, while on Sundays and feast days he celebrated the liturgy in the church.

During the Divine Liturgy, he almost always broke into tears and sighs. Especially at the moment of consecration, his compunction reached its peak. The chanters would sing "We praise Thee…" as slowly as they could, but he would delay five, ten, fifteen minutes or more. So they would repeat the hymn up to five or six times.

Finally, they once approached the church wardens and told them their problem. The wardens in turn conveyed it to the celebrant.

"Father John, you often delay at the time of consecration. The chanters and the people outside wait for you for a long time. Can't you say the prayer more quickly, so there isn't such a gap?"

"How can this be done?"

"It's easy. Where you are lying face down, you can rise, make the sign of the cross over the precious Gifts, say the prayer, and finish."

"I know the prayer, it's written in the service book, but I cannot."

"Why can't you, Father? Forgive us, but it's not difficult!"

"This doesn't depend on me," answered Father John. "As soon as I begin to read the prayer, the Holy Altar is surrounded by divine fire that reaches two or three meters high. So I cannot approach to seal the precious Gifts. I am seized with fear and trembling. I don't know what to do. I fall to the ground, weep, sigh, and implore the Lord to part the flames so I can continue. Then I lift my eyes. If the flames have disappeared, I rise and seal the precious Gifts. If not, then I continue my supplication with tears and sighs until the fire goes out, or another way is found that will allow me not to be burned. Occasionally, the fire goes out and everything becomes as before. Other times the flames part to the right and left forming an arch, so I make the bold move, approach trembling, and seal the precious Gifts."

Hearing these extraordinary things, the Christians didn't bother him again. He was, after all, very devout and exceptionally reverent when celebrating the liturgy. For this reason, faithful from neighboring villages would attend church in his parish, walking for hours to arrive.

Occasionally, a thousand or more faithful would come to the liturgy. And all of them would be moved to compunction and weep. Indeed, at the end of this Divine Mystagogy, the floor of the church would be wet from their tears, as if someone had spilled water!

[26]

"Offering and Being Offered"

An anonymous hesychast, author of the book *The Watchful Mind*, narrates the following wondrous experience:

While celebrating the liturgy with my elder, I saw in a vision the Lord Jesus Christ. He was wearing hierarchical vestments and was officiating according to the order of the Church. Paradoxically, however, he was both "the offerer and the offered." Some from my elder's entourage also participated in the liturgy. Two of them had faces radiant with divine grace, like the faces of angels. Their schema, pectoral cross, and the cross they were holding shone more brightly than lightning!

A deacon was also celebrating with us. At the moment when the deacon was commemorating the names of Christians, Christ compassionately leaned toward him and said: "Let them also be with me in my kingdom."

Seeing the sweetest Jesus before me, I wept with joy and marveled, because I was deemed worthy to enjoy the sight of Him. And when I embraced Him at His most pure chest, I felt myself melting like wax from the great compunction and tears. I then took courage and said to Him weeping: "Remember me, Lord, in Your kingdom." And immediately I heard Jesus with His honey-flowing tongue say to me: "Let it be as you said."

Then I recovered from the vision. That day, however, every time I remembered it, my heart was flooded with compunction.

[9]

A Contemporary Holy Celebrant

Saint Nicholas Planas (+1932), a saint of our days, celebrated the liturgy daily, without interruption, for a period of half a century. During this time, it sometimes happened that he did not have communion bread [*prosphora*]. However, he always managed to obtain it either from the faithful or from the nearby bakeries.

One day, the Orthros service had progressed considerably, but communion bread was nowhere to be found. He sent people to search in the bakeries and among the housewives, who always had some. He also looked in the sanctuary cupboards, in case another priest had left some. But with no result. He became distressed to the point of tears.

At some point, they see him coming out to the royal doors holding a communion bread that was fresh as could be. He had found it on the Holy Altar! "Look, my children, what a sign God has done for me," he said, moved and joyful.

All miracles, he called them signs. He considered them natural, because he had great faith. In the synaxaria we meet ascetics who were served by an angel of the Lord. Very natural then that an angel of the Lord would also serve Papa-Nicholas, the "true ascetic living in the world."

Several of his parishioners, mainly small children, saw him literally levitating when he celebrated the liturgy.

"The fame of Papa-Nicholas," narrates a respected woman, "had spread throughout Athens. Once, on Christmas Eve, I set out with my grandchildren to receive communion from his sanctified hands.

"At that time, Vouliagmeni was still a wilderness. Twenty humble houses scattered here and there and fields all around. In place of today's church, there was an old Byzantine chapel, small as a cubicle, low and dimly lit.

"Other families had come with their children too. At one point, when Papa-Nicholas appeared at the royal doors holding the Holy Chalice, my grandchild shouted:

"'Grandmother, the priest is walking in the air!'

"'Be quiet,' I tell him, while crossing myself. 'How can he be walking in the air?'

"'I see him too,' shouted another child. 'He's not touching the ground.'

"At the 'With fear…' all of us women and children approached to receive communion. Papa-Nicholas had not heard anything, or if he had, he paid no attention at all.

"From then on, I always came here to receive communion. And every time, it was impossible not to hear children shouting:

"'The priest is walking in the air!'

"In 1920, on Christmas Day, the saint was celebrating the liturgy at St. John in Vouliagmeni. When he came out to give communion to the faithful, a woman with her baby approached. After giving communion to the little one, he gave it to a girl, Julia, to hold it.

"Julia, while holding it, turned and looked at the priest. Then she almost dropped the child from her hands.

"'Be careful! What's wrong with you?' the woman shouted to her.

"'I see the priest standing on a cloud,' she answered ecstatically.

"Another time, while the saint was celebrating the liturgy at Prophet Elisha's church, this happened: An eight-year-old child comes out pale from the sanctuary and says to his mother:

"'Mom, Papa-Nicholas is this high from the ground!'

"And he showed her half a cubit with his little hand."

[21]

Liturgical Experiences

Hieromonk Joachim Spetsieris (1858-1943) narrates the following experiences from his time at the monastery of St. Sabbas in Jerusalem:

"On the fourth Sunday of Great Lent in 1888, Hieromonk Germanos was celebrating the liturgy in the katholikon. He was a model of a true monk, simple, innocent, guileless, gentle, and humble.

"After the Great Entrance, when he came out to the royal doors to bless the congregation, his face appeared to me like a fiery flame.

"'What happened to Father Germanos?' I asked Fr. Cyril, thinking that something unpleasant had happened to him.

"'Be quiet,' he tells me, 'he is elevated by divine grace. Spiritually, he no longer lives in the world, he is in heaven. Don't you see that he moves mechanically, as if he's absent-minded? This happens every time he celebrates the liturgy.'

Hieromonk Joachim Spetsieris

"When I became a priest, one day I asked Father Germanos:

"'Father Germanos, I have read that in earlier times many priests, when they performed the Great Entrance carrying the precious Gifts, did not touch the ground. Are there such priests today?'

"'Do not doubt,' he told me, 'lest something like this might happen to you too!'

"Indeed, the following Sunday I was the celebrant. So when I came out for the Great Entrance carrying the Holy Gifts, I was lifting my feet because I couldn't find solid ground to step on. Later, Father Germanos visited me in my cell and asked me:

"'Why today, at the time of the Great Entrance, were you lifting your feet?'

"'I don't know what happened to me, I couldn't find solid ground to step on.'

"'Exactly. You were in the air, because divine angels were holding you. So believe and do not investigate, because the Mystery of the Divine Eucharist is great.'

"'Only during the Great Entrance do the divine angels hold the celebrant in the air?'

"'Yes, because then he carries the precious Gifts upon himself. When he sets them down, then grace works on his spirit, which elevates it to the luminous and heavenly world.'"

[49]

A Wondrous Sign

Saint Savvas, a contemporary saint (1862-1948), protector and patron of Kalymnos, celebrated the Divine Liturgy with perfect devotion to the mystery.

Saint Savvas the New of Kalymnos

Many times, he would concelebrate and converse with saints, sometimes even with the Three Hierarchs, while simultaneously being surrounded by choirs of angels. During the moment of Holy Communion, as observed by his fellow celebrants or other faithful, the Holy Chalice would swell and overflow, yet the Holy Communion would not spill.

Niki Koutelaina, who later became Nun Salome, once saw the saint during the Proskomidi (Preparation of the Gifts) greatly elevated, while angelic hosts stood around him. She also noticed that the Holy Chalice was swelling.

The woman was frightened but said nothing. Later, she revealed to Saint Savvas what she had seen. However, he told her:

"Oh, my child, by God! Do not tell this to anyone!"

[44]

Charismatic States

From 1931, the blessed Elder Ieronymos, abbot of the Simonopetra Monastery on Mount Athos (1871–1957), served as a spiritual father at one of the monastery's dependencies, the Ascension in Athens. This was seen as divine providence, allowing his sanctity to shine in the capital and guiding many souls toward salvation.

As a liturgist, he was characterized by unwavering devotion to the mystery of the Divine Eucharist. When he celebrated the liturgy, he appeared disembodied. Many children attending his sacred services saw him elevated a span above the ground and exclaimed: "The elder is flying! Look, he's not touching the ground!"

A nun also witnessed him walking in the air during the Great Entrance, rather than descending the steps of the northern gate of the sanctuary. Another nun recounted that during the Divine Liturgy, they often saw him standing before the Holy Altar, elevated a span above the ground.

Little Venetia, who later became a nun, once saw him during a liturgy with her innocent eyes surrounded by angels at the Holy Altar. During those days, his appearance was transfigured, and for a long time, she did not enter the church but watched in awe from the doorway.

One rainy winter night, when heavy rain was falling, Elder Ieronymos was informed that a sick person needed Holy Communion. He immediately left for their home, carrying the Precious Mysteries. Remarkably, despite the downpour, he did not get wet at all on his journey!

[28]

Concelebrant of Saints

Saint George Karslides (1901–1959), originally from Pontus, settled in the region of Drama in 1930, where he became a hieromonk and confessor, engaging in significant spiritual work. As a celebrant of the Divine Liturgy, he experienced supernatural states, which were the result of his holy life. He advised his spiritual children: "Strengthen your faith and try to focus on what is happening during the Divine Liturgy so that you may be deemed worthy to witness the majesty of God—the Holy Spirit descending upon the Holy Altar."

Before celebrating the liturgy, he would rise around midnight to pray and prepare for the great mystery. Tireless and reverent, he stood before the Holy Altar like a burning candle. On one occasion, while commemorating names at the Proskomidi (Preparation of the Gifts), a Christian heard faint and unpleasant voices mockingly repeating the names—these were demons trying to disrupt his prayers.

During the Proskomidi, he would commemorate numerous names of both the living and the departed. He would sometimes note specific names and discreetly inform their relatives about their problems or how they had passed away, encouraging them to hold memorial services, liturgies, and acts of charity.

In a vigil at Saint Minas Church in Thessaloniki, his spiritual children witnessed him mystically co-celebrating with the parish priest, despite being physically absent. This miraculous presence was intended to strengthen them during their vigil.

Saint George Karslides

Father George often communicated with the invisible spiritual world, especially with saints during divine worship. He frequently co-celebrated with saints, humbly saying: "I rarely celebrate alone. Today we had such-and-such saint co-celebrating." During one liturgy, a loud noise was heard from the sanctuary, and afterward, his face appeared transfigured and radiant. He explained: "We had heavenly visitors—Saint Minas, Saint George, Saint Nicholas…"

At another liturgy's conclusion, he emotionally remarked: "We had guests—Saint Nicholas and Saint John; a strict guest was the Honorable Forerunner (Saint John the Baptist)." When censing St. John's icon, his hand trembled out of reverence.

When co-celebrating with saints, he would often commemorate them during dismissal with indescribable joy and emotion. On the eve of the Greco-Italian war, he wept continuously. When asked why he was crying, he replied: "I am orphaned; the Panagia (Virgin Mary) has left with Saint George to go to the front."

Devout Christians often saw him elevated above the ground during liturgy. In one nighttime service, while reading the Gospel, he was seen hovering above the floor. In another liturgy during the Great Entrance, he was seen walking in mid-air before stopping in the center of the church a span above the ground and finally touching down as he entered the sanctuary.

On one occasion, after witnessing such events, a visitor recounted them to other faithful. The elder called him over and sternly slapped him while saying: "Whatever you see must not be told to others!"

After one mystical service, a woman told him: "I saw you shining brightly." To this, he humbly replied: "Am I worthy to shine? Christ is worthy. Perhaps His radiance fell upon me."

[29]

The Heavenly Deacon

Father Athanasius Chamakiotis (+1967), the humble priest of Nerantziotissa in Marousi, was celebrating the liturgy one day in the chapel of the Panagia.

A woman from the congregation, E.M., who was standing near the sanctuary, saw a blonde deacon in a white vestment serving Father Athanasius at the Holy Altar. The deacon always stood to his right.

During the Divine Liturgy, the deacon never left the sanctuary. The woman thought he must have been newly ordained and that the priest was teaching him the liturgical order.

The liturgy ended, and the congregation left. However, she stayed behind, curious to find out who the deacon was. Father Athanasius finished consuming the Holy Gifts and left, but the deacon did not come out of the sanctuary.

The woman then opened the curtain to look inside but saw no one. The deacon had disappeared, and there was no other exit!

When she later recounted the incident to Father Athanasius, he simply and humbly replied: "These things happen, my child, but don't tell anyone."

[7]

Wondrous Vision of God

Papa-Tychon, the renowned Russian hesychast of Kapsala on Mount Athos (+1968), had unique practices during the Divine Liturgy. When he celebrated, he instructed the chanter to stand outside the small chapel, in the narrow corridor, and chant "Lord, have mercy" from there. He preferred to be entirely alone, allowing him to move freely in prayer.

During the Cherubic Hymn, Papa-Tychon would be transported to heavenly realms and remain there for twenty to thirty minutes. The chanter had to repeat the hymn many times until the Great Entrance.

"What did you see and hear, Elder, during those thirty minutes?" he was asked after the liturgy.

The Elder would respond in his charming, broken Greek:

Papa Tychon

"Cherubim-Seraphim glorified God. I fly—oh, oh, oh! During the Cherubic Hymn, guardian angel lift me up. After half hour, guardian angel brings me down... My, my, I celebrate liturgy."

Papa-Tychon communed daily from the Holy Bread. He himself never chanted; he always celebrated the liturgy. [39, 51]

Experiences of a Humble Priest

Father Dimitris Gagastathis (1902-1975), a simple and holy cleric of our century, experienced divine visions during his liturgical service. He recounts:

"Once, during the Great Entrance, as I approached the royal doors, I saw to my left a beautiful child who vanished like a shadow. At the same time, there was a noise from the oil lamp of the Panagia, which began to sway until the end of the liturgy. During a night liturgy at the church of the Archangels, at the time of the doxology, I saw that same child standing in front of the Proskomidi, and then vanishing again like smoke.

"On the feast day of the Holy Spirit, I celebrated the liturgy at the Holy Trinity Monastery of Meteora. What a blessing from God! That liturgy will remain unforgettable to me. During the Great Entrance, a woman descended from the left, a man with a small child from the right, while a multitude of other children followed the precious Gifts.

"Something similar happened on August 8, 1954. At five in the morning, I set out for the village of Ardani. I walked and chanted devotional hymns to thank the Lord and the Theotokos. Arriving at the village church, I began

Orthros, and then entered the Divine Liturgy with spiritual joy and exultation. Then this wonderful thing happened:

"All children 12 years old and younger who were in the church saw two large ladders in the sanctuary, on which children bathed in light were ascending and descending. When I read the Gospel, the Holy Altar was filled with children. During the Great Entrance, the church caretaker saw a woman descending from the left ladder and a man with a small child from the right, while a multitude of children followed the transfer of the precious Gifts."

Sometimes Father Dimitris experienced disturbances from demons during the Divine Liturgy:

"Once," he narrates, "while celebrating the liturgy, I heard noises outside. I went out, and what did I see! The devils were building an apartment building. One was holding a trowel, another a shovel… I made the sign of the cross, and everything disappeared.

"Another time, while celebrating the liturgy at night, they entered the church and began overturning the chairs. Their leader even entered the sanctuary, closed the small window, and grabbed me by the throat to strangle me. I invoked the Holy Archangels, and immediately they vanished.

"The demons, by God's permission, enter the church and put thoughts in the faithful. But as soon as the chanters sing the Cherubic Hymn and the priest comes out for the Great Entrance, they immediately leave."

In December 1968, while Father Dimitris was celebrating the liturgy, among the congregation was a 14-year-old girl tormented by Satan. During the Cherubic Hymn, she suddenly let out a terrible cry and fell down as if dead. The faithful became concerned. But in a few minutes, they lifted her up in good condition, restored to her senses. At the end of the Divine Liturgy, a Paraklesis (Supplication Service) was held, and the girl left the church very different.

Every time Father Dimitris celebrated the liturgy in his village church, the Holy Archangels, the Holy Altar would emit a sweet fragrance. This also happened occasionally in other churches. The fragrance would appear mainly after the Great Entrance, when he placed the precious Mysteries on the Holy Altar. Other times it would appear during the invocation of the Holy Spirit, at the "Thine own of Thine own..."

He often placed cotton under the antimension before beginning the Divine Liturgy, and when finishing, the cotton would be fragrant with myrrh. Many people witnessed this fact and were deeply moved and strengthened in their faith. The aroma from the Holy Altar strengthened the celebrant and comforted him. Sometimes it emerged so abundantly that he found it difficult to breathe. Once, the fragrance rose like a small pillar of smoke and filled the entire church.

When Father Dimitris asked Father Philotheos Zervakos for his opinion, he replied:

"We should not doubt that this is an extraordinary miracle. Most certainly, the fragrance comes from the sacrifice of Jesus Christ, who as a Lamb is slain upon the Holy Altar for our sins. However, it may also come from the holy relics that are beneath the Holy Altar or from the consecration relics."

[42]

The Gift of Prayer

Starets Sampson (+1979) encouraged his spiritual children to persistently ask God for the gift of prayer, saying: "Teach me, Lord, to pray. I do not know how to pray."

"Sometimes," the starets added, "this secret is revealed to us during the Divine Liturgy when we receive communion.

Starets Sampson the Confessor

"I knew a priest who could not learn to pray. Once, at the moment he was receiving communion, he took the Body of Christ with his left hand, placed it on his right hand, and began to read, as usual, the prayer: 'I believe, Lord, and I confess…' When he finished, while tears were flowing from his eyes, he began to fervently implore: 'Teach me, Lord, to pray. I have not yet learned to pray. I only read the prayers.'

"Immediately, as he himself recounted, his face was illuminated by an invisible light and within him another mind opened. He then began to read for a second time the 'I believe, Lord…' without lifting his eyes from the Master's Body. The deacon approached him and said: 'Father, the people are waiting.'

"The communion hymn had ended, but the priest, no matter how hard he tried, could not recover himself. He stood as if lost, like a pillar of salt. And this was because he understood what prayer is. He felt that he was resurrected. From then on, he wept incessantly. And never again could he look upon the most pure Body of the Lord without tears." [50]

"Things on High Celebrate Together with Things Below"

"When the Divine Liturgy is celebrated down on earth, another liturgy is also celebrated in heaven."

This is mentioned by the charismatic Starets Sampson in his "Teachings," where he also narrates the following incident:

"Once, in the katholikon (main church) of a monastery, during the celebration of the Divine Liturgy, a monk was serving and praying at the same time. At one moment, as he looked up, he saw the heavens opened and a Holy Altar. There, three hierarchs were kneeling before it, while nearby stood a choir of indescribable beauty.

"A Divine Liturgy was being celebrated, and it was being officiated by holy hierarchs like Basil the Great, Gregory the Theologian, and John Chrysostom.

"The monk stood gazing as if he were turned to marble. When the others saw him after the liturgy, still standing motionless and soaked with tears, they carefully took him by the hand and led him to his cell."

[50]

Concelebrant of the Holy Trinity

Saint Iakovos Tsalikis (+1991), abbot of Saint David's Monastery, experienced wondrous experiences during all sacred services, but especially during the Divine Liturgy.

When he celebrated the liturgy, he shone with purity and magnificence. Often, during the Great Entrance or at the Proskomidi, people saw him not touching the ground, but standing and walking in the air. Many times he beheld angels and archangels on the Holy Altar holding the Body of the Lord.

"People," he would say, "are blind and do not see what happens inside the church during the Divine Liturgy."

Saint Iakovos (Tsalikis) of Evia

Once, while celebrating, he had difficulty beginning the Great Entrance due to the wonders he was seeing. The chanter kept repeating: "As we receive the King of all." Suddenly, he felt someone pushing him from the shoulder and guiding him to the Proskomidi. He thought it was the chanter, but when he turned, he saw a huge wing of an archangel guiding him to proceed with the Great Entrance.

"What happens in the sanctuary during the liturgy! During the Cherubic Hymn, angels ascend and descend, and I often feel their wings hitting my shoulders… Sometimes I can't bear it and sit in the chair. The other priests think something's wrong with me, but they don't sense what I see and hear."

"Tonight, my child," he once revealed to a monk, "I was co-celebrating with saints and angels at indescribable Altars. When I die, tell them that an elder co-celebrated every night and lived with the Holy Trinity."

During the Proskomidi, Fr. Iakovos often saw the spiritual state of the deceased he commemorated. He said that souls would pass before him, begging to be commemorated. Once, he forgot to commemorate his mother, and she appeared to him, saying with complaint that he had not remembered her that day.

Something similar happened with Archbishop Makarios of Cyprus. As Fr. Iakovos finished the Proskomidi and started towards the Holy Altar, he saw the late archbishop standing to his right, palms cupped as priests do when receiving communion, as if asking for his own portion.

[15, 43]

Who Wounded Him?

The following incident, which was also narrated by Fr. Iakovos, happened one Good Friday.

An elderly woman went to light the oil lamps in a small chapel of her village. Out of curiosity, she looked inside the sanctuary, and what did she see! On the Holy Altar sat a young man, about thirty years old.

He had wounds on his palms and feet, as well as a wound on his side, from which blood was flowing.

"Who are you who dares to sit on the Holy Altar?" asked the woman, astonished.

"I always sit here, this is my place," answered the young man.

"Who wounded you so?"

"You wounded me with your sins."

Indeed, the elderly woman was deemed worthy to see the Lord Himself, because she was in a state of repentance at that time.

[15]

Flames of Fire

Saint Porphyrius (+1991), the well-known contemporary saintly figure, was also a "heaven-ascending" celebrant, as revealed by the following incident.

Once, when he was celebrating the liturgy at Saint Nicholas in Kallisia, dozens of faithful saw countless fiery flames coming out from the roof of the church and ascending to heaven.

Saint Porphyrius

Everyone was speechless. They could not believe their eyes. Each one gave their own explanation for the event, so they asked the elder what these fiery flames might be. And he humbly attributed the phenomenon to the faith of others:

"It's nothing, blessed ones," he answered laconically. "The great faith of the chanters."

[20]

A Voice from the Stole

A contemporary hieromonk from the desert of Mount Athos narrates:

"I was once celebrating the liturgy, newly ordained as a priest, in a remote chapel. Our venerable elder and a brother monk constituted the entire congregation.

"When I reached the exclamation 'Peace be to all' and having the elder in front of me, I thought: 'How can I say "Peace be to all" and bless the elder, since I receive grace from him?'

"Then I hear a voice from the stole saying to me:

"'You are not the one blessing. I am the one blessing!'"

(Oral narration of the hermit)

Priestly Concelebration

Archimandrite Fr. Joel Giannakopoulos (+1966) was a wise and holy priestly figure. Three years after his repose, on October 19, 1969 (the feast day of Prophet Joel), a vigil was held in memory of the blessed Fr. Joel at the chapel of the Orthodox Christian Society "Three Hierarchs" in Athens. Concelebrating were Archimandrites Fr. Agathangelos Michailidis (+1991), Fr. Epiphanios Theodoropoulos (+1989), and Fr. Meletios Kalamaras (now Metropolitan of Nikopolis).

Father Joel Giannakopoulos

Toward the end of the Divine Liturgy, during the communion hymn, several faithful spiritual children of Fr. Joel witnessed a strange vision. A luminous throne appeared in the middle of the church, in the place of the chandelier, as if made of a bright cloud, upon which Fr. Joel was seated. The throne moved above the heads of the crowd, who were watching the Divine Liturgy with compunction and awe. Then it disappeared, and Fr. Joel, dressed in his priestly vestments, appeared among his three celebrating priest friends.

This event was interpreted by the congregation as an indication of Fr. Joel's holiness, but also as a confirmation of our Church's belief that departed pious priests descend to our churches during the Divine Liturgy and concelebrate with their beloved living priests.

[23]

PART IV

WORTHY AND UNWORTHY

Communion of the Apostles (14th century fresco)
Church of St. Nicholas Orphanos, Thessaloniki, Greece

The Disobedient Monk-Martyr

On October 15, our Church honors the memory of an anonymous martyr monk.

This monk lived in a skete in Egypt, and for several years was obedient to an elder. However, through the envy of the evil demon, he abandoned his obedience and left his elder's guidance without any reasonable cause that might harm his soul. He even disregarded the penance that his elder had imposed on him.

So he left and went down to Alexandria. But there he was seized by the pagan ruler,[11] who removed his monastic habit and pressured him to sacrifice to idols. When he could not be persuaded to do this by any means, the ruler first ordered him to be mercilessly beaten with whips, and then to be beheaded by the sword. And so it happened. The pagans seized the monk, cut off his head, and threw his body outside the city to be eaten by dogs.

However, some pious Christians came at night and took it. They anointed it with myrrh, wrapped it in sheets, and placed it in a reliquary. Then they placed it in the sanctuary of a church in the city to be honored as a martyr's relic.

But every time the Divine Liturgy was celebrated, and the deacon proclaimed, "All catechumens, depart.

11 The story takes place during a period of Christian persecution, most likely during the persecution that occurred in Alexandria under Maximinus, between 308 and 311, during which many monks were also martyred.

Catechumens, depart," everyone would see the reliquary leaving the sanctuary by itself! Without being touched by human hands, it would reach the narthex of the church and remain there until dismissal. Then it would return by itself back to the sanctuary!

Everyone was amazed by what was happening. One of the discerning fathers learned of this and asked God to give him an explanation.

The cause of the miracle was soon revealed to him. An angel appeared before him and said:

"Why are you amazed and perplexed by what is happening? Did not the apostles of Christ, as you know, receive authority 'to bind and to loose'? And from them their successors, and so on? This brother, who was deemed worthy to shed his blood for Christ and yet is not permitted to be in the sanctuary during the bloodless sacrifice, know that an angel drives him to the narthex. For a while, he was a disciple of your fellow ascetic, he abandoned his obedience. And when his elder reasonably gave him a penance, he left him and departed, still bound by the penance. And as a martyr, he received the martyr's crown. But being bound by his elder's penance, he cannot be inside the sanctuary when the Divine Liturgy is celebrated. Unless the elder who bound him releases him from the penance."

When that holy ascetic learned these things, he took his staff, went to the martyr's elder, and told him everything. Then he took him and they went down to Alexandria together.

They went to the church where the martyr's relic was kept. They opened the reliquary containing the martyr's body, and they both gave him forgiveness. Then, after venerating him, they stood and prayed, glorifying God.

From then on, when the Divine Liturgy was celebrated, the martyr monk remained unmoved in his place within the sanctuary.

[14]

Approach Worthily

In the 4th century, in the deserts of Thebes and Nitria, renowned and spiritually-gifted ascetics lived. One of them was the presbyter Eulogius. When he performed the liturgy, he received such a gift of knowledge that he could understand the spiritual state of each monk who approached to receive communion, and he would advise them accordingly:

"How dare you approach the Holy Mysteries with a defiled mind? You had thoughts of fornication this night."

"And you," he would say to another, "were thinking that there is no difference between the sinner and the righteous when approaching divine grace."

"And you," he observed of a third, "doubted whether the Divine Communion would sanctify you."

"Therefore, distance yourselves from the Holy Mysteries and repent wholeheartedly so that your sins may be forgiven, and you may become worthy of Communion with Christ. If you do not cleanse your souls, you cannot approach the grace of God."

Another presbyter, Piammonas, who lived near Diolkopolis, very humble and virtuous, continuously saw visions.

One day, while offering the bloodless sacrifice, he saw an angel standing at the right side of the Holy Altar, writing in a book the names of the brothers who approached to receive communion. He also saw the angel erasing the names of some monks who had not come to the assembly. These monks died after thirteen days!

Piammonas was tormented greatly by demons, who made him so weak that he could not stand and perform the liturgy. However, once a holy angel approached him, took him by the hand, strengthened him, and led him back healthy before the Holy Altar.

[18]

The Deacon's Offense

Every time Saint Epiphanius, Archbishop of Constantia in Cyprus (4th century), offered the bloodless sacrifice and said, "make this bread…," if he did not see a certain vision, he would not complete the Divine Liturgy.

What kind of vision was this? Perhaps it was the movement of the wooden dove that hung above the holy table in the churches of that era. Or perhaps it was some ineffable action or appearance of the Holy Spirit at the time of consecration, something that happened to other worthy celebrants as well.

During one liturgy, Saint Epiphanius repeated the prayer of consecration three times, but did not see the vision. And while he was tearfully beseeching God to reveal the cause, he glanced at the deacon, who was standing to his left holding the fan, and noticed that he had leprosy on his forehead.

He immediately understood that this was the cause. So he took the fan from his hands and said to him with gentleness:

"Go, my child, to your home and do not receive communion today."

Then he repeated the prayer, and immediately saw the vision. After the dismissal, he called the deacon to examine

Saint Epiphanius, Archbishop of Constantia,
Church of Saint Nicholas tis Stegis (of the Roof), Cyprus

him and learn about his spiritual condition. The deacon then confessed that the previous night he had been intimate with his wife.

Using this occasion, the saint called all the clergy and admonished them:

"Those of you, my children, who have been deemed worthy to receive the gift of priesthood, must keep yourselves pure from every defilement 'of flesh and spirit,' in order to worthily perform the Divine Mysteries."

[30]

The Purifying Divine Power

Abba Mark the Egyptian remained enclosed for thirty years, never leaving his cell at all. For his sake, the presbyter of Scetis would go there and celebrate the Divine Liturgy.

The devil, annoyed by the patience and virtue of the holy man, wanted to trouble him. So he sent a demon-possessed person, who said to him: "Abba, your presbyter stinks of sin. Therefore, do not let him into your cell again."

"Everyone," answered the holy man, "leaves their impurity outside. Only you have brought it inside. Don't forget what the Scripture says: 'Judge not, that ye be not judged.' Even if my presbyter is sinful, God will save him."

When the priest came again, the abba welcomed him with great joy. And God, seeing the innocence of the elder, showed him a revealing sign:

While the priest was preparing to stand before the holy table to perform the Divine Mystery, an angel of the Lord descended and placed his hand on his head. From that moment, the priest became like a pillar of fire.

Astonished by the vision, the holy man heard a voice saying to him: "Why are you amazed, man? If an earthly king does not allow his nobles to appear filthy before him, how much more will the divine power cleanse from every stain the ministers of the Holy Mysteries when they stand before the King of glory?"

[16]

The Celebrant, a Conduit of Grace

A related incident is the following:

A presbyter used to visit a reclusive hermit in his hermitage and perform the Divine Liturgy there.

However, once a visitor slandered the presbyter to the hermit with a multitude of accusations. The hermit was influenced and felt antipathy towards the presbyter. So when he came to celebrate the liturgy, the hermit did not open the door for him.

Immediately, then, the hermit hears a voice saying to him: "Humans have taken away from me the right of judgment."

At the same time, he went into ecstasy and saw the following vision:

A leper was standing over a golden well, drawing crystal-clear water with a golden bucket. The hermit, although thirsty, hesitated to drink because the leper was drawing it.

He then hears a second voice saying to him: "Why don't you drink? Don't you see what vessel the leper is using? Besides, he only draws it and then empties it."

When the hermit came to his senses, he understood the meaning of the vision, and after calling the presbyter, he asked him to perform the Divine Liturgy as always.

[16]

Faces Bright and Black

Regarding our preparation before approaching the mystery of the Divine Eucharist, we read the following in *The Sayings of the Desert Fathers*:

There was a holy bishop who, whenever he came out at the beautiful gate to commune the people, used to see some approaching with a pitch-black face or swollen eyes. As soon as these ones received the Immaculate Mysteries, they were burned.

Yet there were others who approached with pure white attire and a bright face, who received the Body of the Lord with attention and piety. The Holy Communion made these ones even brighter.

The bishop entreated God to explain this mystery to him. Then an angel of the Lord appeared to his and said:

"Those who commune with a radiant face and white garment are chaste and pure, righteous and compassionate. They approach with a pure conscience, and it is for this reason that the divine grace overshadows them. On the contrary, those who appear black as coal are men immersed in the mire of carnal desires. Those with irritated and swollen eyes are wicked and unjust, spiteful and insatiate. Not only are these ones not benefited by the Divine Communion, but rather they are condemned, because they dare to approach with a guilty conscience, without repentance and preparation."

From that point forward the virtuous bishop preached repentance to his flock and forbade the unworthy ones from approaching Holy Communion.

[55]

Do Not Trifle with Sacred Matters

A characteristic case of divine punishment to an unworthy priest is narrated by Palladius in the *Lausiac History*:

"I once visited Saint Macarius of Alexandria. Outside his cell, I found a village presbyter lying down. His head was completely eaten away by cancer. Even the bone at the top was visible. He had come to the holy man to be healed, but the holy man did not want to see him. I approached him then and said:

"'Please, have mercy on this man and give him some answer.'

"'He is unworthy of being healed,' the abba answered me. 'God has sent him punishment because, while he was fornicating, he was celebrating the liturgy. However, if you wish him to be healed, persuade him to abstain from the Divine Liturgy. Then God will have mercy on him.'

"I immediately approached the sick priest, spoke with him, and he promised me with an oath that he would stop performing priestly functions. Then the holy man received him and said to him:

"'Do you believe that God exists?'

"'I believe.'

"'Were you perhaps able to play with Him?'

"'No.'

"'If then you recognize your sin and the punishment that God gave you for it, make sure to correct yourself.'

"Immediately, the guilty one confessed his sin and promised that he would not do it again nor would he celebrate the liturgy anymore, but would return to the rank of the laity.

"Then the holy man placed his hand on him, healed him, and let him go back to his homeland."

[40]

The Eagle

When they celebrated the Divine Eucharist in Scetis, the Holy Spirit would descend like an eagle over the offering, but no one else could see it except the clergy.

One day, a monk asked the deacon for a favor, but he spoke to him abruptly: "I don't have time now, go away!"

So when they celebrated the liturgy the next time, none of the clergy saw the eagle descending at its usual time. Then the presbyter addresses the deacon and says to him: "What's happening? Why didn't the eagle appear today? For this to happen, either I am at fault or you are. Step aside for a moment, and if it descends now when you are away from the Altar, it means you are at fault; otherwise, it will be me."

As soon as the deacon moved away, immediately the eagle hovered over the holy table! After the divine liturgy, the presbyter asks the deacon:

"Tell me, what did you do?"

"I don't remember sinning in anything," he answered, "except for this: A brother came and asked me for a favor, and I told him that I didn't have time."

"Surely, this is the reason the eagle didn't descend," replied the presbyter, "because you grieved the brother."

The deacon then left and went to make prostration to the brother and ask for forgiveness.

[45]

The Two Widows

A bishop was informed about two Christian widows that they were not living with modesty. He then asked God to inform him about this matter so that he could decide what to do.

Indeed, God granted His servant what he asked for. During the Divine Liturgy, when the faithful were receiving communion, the bishop could see on each person's face the sins they had committed and that tormented them.

Some faces appeared as if stained with soot. Others looked completely burned, with bloodshot and inflamed eyes. However, there were also Christians who had a bright appearance and snow-white clothes.

When the first group received communion, he saw them surrounded by flames and burning. In contrast, for the others, the Pearl they received became a powerful light that enveloped their entire body with its radiance.

After the men, the bishop began to administer the precious Gifts to the women. And in them, he observed the same images. Some faces appeared black, others blood-red, others inflamed, and others pure white.

At some point, those two ill-reputed widows approached to receive communion. He then sees them dressed in pure white garments and having bright and modest faces. When they received the Immaculate Mysteries, he saw them bathed in a dazzling light.

The liturgy ended, and the bishop began to pray again, asking God for an explanation of the revelations. Then a holy angel appears before him.

"Are the things that people say about those two women true or false?" the bishop asks him.

"Yes, they are all true."

"But why when they received communion did they have bright faces, wear snow-white garments, and shine with dazzling light?"

"This happened because the women became aware of their sinful life, repented with tears, sighs, almsgiving, and confession, and promised not to fall into the same sins again. Thus, God forgave them, and since then, they have been living with modesty and piety."

[45]

The Ill-Tempered Female Ascetics

In the mid-6th century, two virgins were practicing asceticism on the outskirts of Rome. They came from an aristocratic family and lived near the monastery of Saint Benedict. A pious Christian took care to provide them with whatever they needed. However, with the arrogance of their aristocratic origin, they daily mocked, insulted, and offended that good man.

At some point, he could no longer endure their behavior, which had become truly unbearable, and went to complain to Saint Benedict. After this, the saint called the two women and scolded them severely:

"Correct yourselves and restrain your tongues, or else I will not give you communion."

But they did not change at all. And unfortunately, after a short time, they both died.

They were buried inside the church, as was customary then. However, from the day of their burial, something terrible began to happen: At every Divine Liturgy, at the moment when the deacon called those who would not receive communion to leave the church, a pious woman — who had served as their nurse and always brought offerings for their souls — saw the two virgins rising from their graves and going out!

When this happened several times, the woman runs crying to Saint Benedict, falls at his feet, and reveals to him the terrifying vision.

Immediately, the saint gives her an offering and tells her:

"Take it to the priest and ask him to celebrate the liturgy for the repose of their souls. This way, they will be released from the penance of excommunication."

And indeed, this is what happened! The priest celebrated the Divine Liturgy for their sake with the offering of Saint Benedict, and from then on, the woman never saw them leaving the church again.

[16]

The Punishment and the Redemption

In the years of the Eastern Roman Emperor Constantine the Younger,[12] a multitude of Scythians by his order set out for the East. Eventually, they reached Trebizond. Among them was someone bound in chains, because he had within him an entire legion of evil spirits. The other Scythians watched him day and night, fearing that the demons might throw him into fire and burn him, or drown him in water, or push him into some abyss.

Before becoming possessed, this Scythian, from his youth, had done the will of demons and lived a dissolute life. Once, however, he committed a terrible sacrilege: in Constantinople, where he had gone with other compatriots, he visited a church. There, although unbaptized and unclean, he dared to approach the Holy Chalice at the time of Divine Communion and receive it! At that very moment, he was delivered to the merciless demons, who from then on began to torture him ruthlessly.

12 This is probably Constantine X Ducas (1059-1067), successor to Isaac I Comnenus.

So, in this condition, he arrived in Trebizond. His companions, learning about the many miracles of Saint Eugenius, brought him to his church.

Meanwhile, the satanic legion made him convulse and foam at the mouth. "How did you dare," the demons threatened him, "to receive Christ, since you are ours? We will destroy you in the most cruel way! No one will save you from our hands!"

But while the foul demons were boasting and threatening, what does the quick helper of humans, the glorious Eugenius, do? He beseeches the merciful Master to have compassion on His creature and deliver it from the tyranny of Satan. And with his supplications, he moves the all-merciful Lord.

As the possessed man stood before the relics of the saint, he went into ecstasy. It seemed to him that he saw Christ descending from heaven into the church. There, after reminding him of the profane acts he had committed since his youth, He began to rebuke him severely.

"With all these transgressions of yours," the Lord concluded, "you have grieved me very much. You are not worthy of mercy. However, for the sake of my beloved Eugenius, I have pitied you and will show you mercy."

And turning to the martyr, who stood beside Him pleadingly, He continued: "Heal him, Eugenius, since he has sought your protection."

Immediately, Jesus disappeared.

The saint then said to the possessed man: "You suffered this evil because you received the Immaculate Mysteries while being unbaptized and immersed in sins."

The Scythian came out of his ecstasy. He then saw, physically now, fire coming out from the holy relics, entering his mouth and consuming—so it seemed to him—his insides.

Those who were nearby could see with their own eyes the power of Saint Eugenius, who was tormenting and punishing the evil demons with authority, violently driving them out of the wretched man.

The Scythian was foaming and sweating and convulsing, until he was completely freed from the unclean spirits.

Peaceful now and undisturbed, he loathed his old life, and never ceased to thank the miracle-working martyr who had helped him.

[3]

The Celebrant Angel

In Cyprus, in the village of Trachiades, ten years before the fall of the island (1571), there lived an unworthy priest.

With the cooperation of the evil one, he had been led astray and had learned the magical art to perfection. He had even reached the point of eating and drinking from sacred vessels with prostitutes!

Divine justice, however, soon punished him. As soon as the ruler of the region learned of his conduct, he sentenced him to death. And when the condemned man was led to the middle of the amphitheater, a counselor of the ruler asked him:

"Tell me, defiled one, with what heart, with what lips, with what hands did you dare to approach the Undefiled One? Didn't you tremble lest a thunderbolt burn you, lest the earth swallow you? How did you dare, you who worshiped the devil, to administer the Divine Mysteries to Christians?"

"I swear by the God who is about to damn me," he then answered, "that from the hour I became a magician and sorcerer, I did not perform the liturgy myself. As soon as I entered the Holy Altar, an angel would descend from heaven, tie me behind a column, and he would perform the liturgy. Finally, after giving communion to the people, he would untie me and I would leave."

[1]

The Unrepentant Woman

Once, a woman lived with fasting and prayers. She appeared outwardly devout, but she had much pride and believed she was a saint. She also had so much resentment that, if she quarreled with another woman, not only would she not forgive her, but she did not even want to see her face again.

Once she fell ill and called for her spiritual father, but she did not confess clearly. This is a habit of some superficial Christians, who hide their great sins and reveal only the small ones.

Finally, when the priest brought the Holy Gifts to give her communion, she turned her face to the wall and could not even look at the Divine Pearl. At that same moment, by divine permission, she confessed in a loud voice:

"Just as I, out of pride, did not forgive those who wronged me, but turned away from them, so now the Lord turns His face away from me and does not want to enter my unworthy soul. I will not see Him in the heavenly kingdom, but I will burn in eternal hell!"

And with these words, she passed away.

[1]

"Consuming Fire"

The following account by Father Dimitrios Gagastathis (1902–1975) is astounding, regarding those who partake of the Holy Mysteries unworthily:

"Once, I was called to go and give Holy Communion to an elderly woman, Zoe Gagastathi, 85 years old, who had been bedridden for some time. As soon as I gave her Communion, she cried out: 'The Communion burned me! I'm on fire! Give me water! I'm burning!' She lived only a few more hours, during which she continually shouted: 'I'm burning, poor me!'"

St. Dimitrios Gagastathis

This woman suffered from the demon of slander. Her mouth never stopped judging others. She also suffered from the demon of gluttony. She communed unworthily, and when she died, her mouth remained open — as if she still wanted to speak.

[42]

The Empty Spoon

Elder Iakovos Tsalikis (+1991) once heard the confession of an elderly woman and gave her a penance not to receive communion for three years.

"Why don't you receive communion?" the parish priest asked her one day.

"Father Iakovos gave me a penance," she replied, and told him the reason.

"No, grandmother, don't worry. He is an uneducated monk. I am educated, and I release you from the penance. Come on Sunday and I will give you communion."

However, as the grandmother approached to receive communion, she felt the Holy Spoon empty and cold in her mouth. She did not taste the Divine Communion. This wondrous event was repeated two more Sundays, at which point the woman became concerned and went back to Elder Iakovos.

"My child," he told her, "the penance cannot be released. You must complete the penance I gave you."

In 1987, Father Iakovos heard the confession of a young woman, but forbade her to receive communion. She then visited a certain bishop, who permitted her to receive Holy Communion. However, when she approached to receive communion, the Holy Spoon entered her mouth empty. This strange and wondrous event happened again another time, at which point the young woman became frightened, repented, and went to confess once more to Father Iakovos.

[15]

Wondrous Transformations

"When I give Holy Communion to people," the ever-blessed Elder Iakovos used to say characteristically, "I never look at their faces. But occasionally, a thought comes to me to look at them. Then I see some faces take the form of a dog, an ape, or other animals. Their appearance is terrifying. Yet, I also see some faces that are calm and bright, and after receiving Holy Communion, they shine like the sun."

Once, a fellow priest said to him: "The Holy Communion burned me!"

"It didn't burn me," the elder replied.

On the contrary, he experienced so intensely the partaking of the Lord's Body that he was spiritually and physically renewed.

"Today, when you received Communion," he said to one of his spiritual children, "do you see how you feel? That's how I feel always. Christ is always within me."

[15]

An Unworthy Man on His Deathbed

A Russian priest gives the following personal testimony:

"I was called to hear the confession of and give communion to a seriously ill man. Entering the house, I heard shouting and curses from his room. I wondered who was swearing in such a manner and disturbing the peace that should prevail in these critical hours. However, I was shocked to discover that it was the dying man himself."

"I was thinking about how to communicate with this person who, shortly before dying, was swearing and cursing. After praying, I finally entered his room, determined to do my duty. I first heard his confession, and then gave him communion."

"When I returned to the church, I stopped to arrange the Holy Chalice that I had taken with me. Then I felt a shiver run through me. I discovered that the precious Gifts were still inside, just as when I had set out to go to the sick man. It was as if he had not received communion! The Lord covered both my eyes and those of the dying man, and the transmission of the Lord's Body and Blood did not take place. This man was unworthy to receive communion in his final moments."

[24]

PART V

"A REMEDY FOR DIVERS MALADIES"

The Crucifixion (16th century icon)
by Theophanes the Cretan

Holy Communion and the Demon

Horror, dread, and panic seize the demons when they find themselves before the Body and Blood of the Lord—the Holy Communion. That is why the demon-possessed always writhe and thrash about miserably when they approach the Holy Gifts—something that does *not* happen before the consecration and transformation of the elements.

This, too, is a continual and striking proof that Holy Communion is truly the Body and Blood of Christ.

In the life of Saint Eutychius, Patriarch of Constantinople (6th century), there is a related incident.

In the region of Amasia, where he had been exiled for a time, there was a women's monastery called "of Flavia." Some of the nuns brought to the saint a five-year-old girl who was possessed by a demon and would not go near Holy Communion. Whenever they tried to bring her to commune, she would scream, thrash about, kick, and turn away from the Holy Mysteries in disgust and terror.

The next day was Sunday. The saint would be serving the Divine Liturgy and communing the faithful. He asked them to bring the little girl again.

Indeed, they brought her, and with much force, they managed to get her to open her mouth and receive the Holy Communion. But she immediately let out a wild scream and spat it out onto the ground!

Everyone was horrified. They let the frenzied child go, while the saint gathered the Body and Blood of Christ from the ground with his own mouth. Nevertheless, he instructed them to bring the possessed child back again the next day.

When she arrived, the saint prayed and anointed all her limbs with holy oil. Then he tried to give her Holy Communion again.

The girl sighed deeply, then received Communion calmly and without fear. As soon as she swallowed the Holy Communion, she let out a loud, wild cry, and immediately the evil spirit came out of her mouth.

From that moment, the little girl was completely healed, and everyone glorified the Lord for His power and compassion.

[22]

The Defiled Wine

A woman once lived a life of martyrdom because her husband—who was actually a priest—beat her and cursed her every day. She began searching for an opportunity to separate from him.

The presbytera (priest's wife) shared her pain with a certain friend, and this friend, who was cunning and godless, gave her the following diabolical advice:

"If you want to achieve your goal, give him defiled blood mixed with wine to drink. As soon as he drinks it, he'll go insane, and his madness will be a perfect excuse for you to leave him."

So the presbytera was persuaded, and she prepared that dreadful concoction. But mistakenly, she put it into the bottle where the priest usually kept the wine for the Divine Liturgy.

And so, one day when her husband was preparing to serve the Liturgy, he took the bottle with the defiled wine and celebrated the Divine Liturgy with it—unaware of his wife's wicked scheme.

And here's the miracle! That polluted mixture, by the descent of the Holy Spirit, became the Blood of Christ.

And those who received Holy Communion—beginning with the priest himself—not only did not go insane, but received it "for the cleansing and sanctification of soul and body."

Later, when the presbytera looked for the bottle and couldn't find it, she realized what had happened and was shaken to her core. She quickly went to her spiritual father. There, she confessed her sin with wailing and anguish, believing that not only had the priest and the faithful been defiled, but even the Holy Gifts themselves.

But the spiritual father replied:

"Know this, woman: neither the Holy Gifts nor those who communed were defiled. On the contrary, by the descent of the Holy Spirit, they were sanctified. But that doesn't mean you didn't sin. And if you'll listen to me, you and your priest-husband should leave the world and become monastics. I believe that now this is what will benefit your souls the most."

[53]

Consuming a Snake

On the small island of Psara, the homeland of the hero Kanaris, who burned the Turkish armada, there are no snakes. In earlier times, in the area known as Fidolakos ("snake-pit"), there stood the monastery of Saint Matrona. As the name suggests, the place used to be full of snakes.

Once, during a Divine Liturgy, a small snake fell into the Holy Communion. The priest saw it and was horrified. What could he do? He could not throw it away, because it had been soaked with the Holy Communion. So he was forced to consume it.

The grace of the sacrament protected him, and he suffered no harm—but he was deeply troubled and disturbed in his soul. He was indignant, and with a loud cry, he begged Christ to make the snakes disappear from the island.

The result? To this very day, not a single snake has appeared on Psara. Many times, snakes have been brought over from nearby islands as a test, but as soon as they move three or four meters, they die.

In fact, soil from Fidolakos, if taken to other regions, protects against snakes. Many visitors take soil from that area, bring it to other places, and wherever it is scattered, no snakes appear in that home.

[13]

"For the Healing of Both Soul and Body"

Many of the miraculous healings performed by the beloved modern saint of northern Russia, St. John of Kronstadt (+1908), were accomplished through Holy Communion. His healing power was most often revealed at the moment of the distribution of the Immaculate Mysteries. With the deep faith he inspired, the sick would partake "for the healing of soul and body."

Sermon in Saint Andrew's Cathedral in Kronstadt during the time of Saint John of Kronstadt

Fr. Vasily Sustin recounts that when he was still very young, his father fell gravely ill with laryngeal tuberculosis. Professor Simanovsky declared that the patient had only ten days to live.

At that time, St. John was in Kronstadt. A telegram was sent to him, and he arrived five days later.

"Why didn't you inform me that he was so seriously ill?" he asked. "I would have brought Holy Communion with me."

Then, turning to the sick man, he asked:

"Do you believe that, by the power of Christ, I can help you?"

The man nodded in affirmation. Then the man of God breathed into his mouth three times in the form of the cross. Afterward, he struck the table that held the medicine and said:

"Throw this away. It's useless. But come to Kronstadt so that I can give you the Immaculate Mysteries. I will be waiting for you."

When the doctor heard this, he declared that the patient would die on the way. But the man did indeed travel to Kronstadt, where the saint gave him Holy Communion. He stayed there for two days, during which all his wounds closed up — only his voice remained weak.

When he returned home, the doctor was astonished.

"This," he declared in front of everyone, "is unprecedented. It is a clear and undeniable miracle!"

That "dying man" went on to live another 25 years!

In older biographies of the saint, there is also an account of the healing of an elderly woman after receiving Holy Communion.

"You should receive Communion," Fr. John urged her, "and the Lord will heal you."

"But I'm very old," the woman said, "and that's why I don't think I can be healed."

"It's not our place to know the times and the appointments of God," he answered.

"She has received Communion in the past," her relatives added.[13]

"The first Christians received Communion every day," the saint responded. "And now, when she needs it most, you don't want her to receive it?"

In the end, the woman received Holy Communion and soon recovered.

Also noteworthy is the miraculous healing of Princess Z.N. Yusupova, who had developed sepsis after a premature birth. The saint visited her (as she herself recounts), sat beside her bed, and said:

13 At that time the erroneous view prevailed that it was enough for the faithful to commune only once a year.

"Whether you live or not is in God's hands. But you must prepare for a new life through the reception of the Immaculate Mysteries."

"But, Father," she said, "I'm planning to receive Communion before Pascha."

"Even though Pascha is near," he insisted, "you should not postpone it. I am ready to bring the Holy Gifts right now."

Moved by his insistence, she agreed. After receiving with awareness and joy, she slept for six hours. When she awoke, she was completely healed!

Professor Botkin, who had been treating her, was so struck by the change that he remained silent for a long time. Two tears ran down his face, and then he whispered thoughtfully:

"We humans did not accomplish this healing."

The saint himself also recounted other similar events:

"A man was suffering from a deadly stomach ulcer. For nine days, he had found no relief from the doctors.

"I prayed fervently for him, saying: 'Lord, You are our life! Just as easily as I can think of healing, so easily can You grant it. Heal Your servant Basil from this terrible affliction.' Then I gave him Holy Communion, and he received it with steadfast faith. That very afternoon, he got better, and that night he rose from his bed. The Lord Christ had mercy on him and granted him health… I am amazed by the life-giving power of the Immaculate Mysteries!

"An elderly woman had been coughing up blood. She was extremely weak and hardly ate anything. But after I gave her Communion, she began to recover.

"A young woman was at death's door. She, too, was healed by Holy Communion. Glory to Your life-giving Mysteries, O Lord!"

Finally, the saint—a zealous proclaimer of the Immaculate Mysteries—would not fail to declare their miraculous power with the following exhortation:

"Invite the priest to your home with the Body and Blood of Christ. Believe, as Jairus believed, that your desires will be fulfilled. In my priestly ministry, I have seen many examples of the sick being healed quickly through deep faith, repentance, and Holy Communion."

[4]

The Wonder-Working Remedy

A well-known Russian priest and confessor, Fr. Dimitry Dudko (born in 1922), recorded the account of a mother regarding the miraculous healing of her son through Holy Communion. Here is what she herself said:

Fr. Dimitry Dudko

"Until the age of 14, I took my son to church and he received Communion. After that, he didn't want to go anymore. It was difficult to force him to go to church.

"But from that time on, he began jumping out of bed at night, shouting, trying to grab things, in a state of great agitation. I often consulted doctors. They attributed it to his awkward age and said it would pass. They even prescribed him some pills, but they didn't help at all.

"The nighttime episodes became more and more frequent. Later, they said he had lunar epilepsy and that there was no help for him.

"Yet, he had excellent health and was very strong. His academic performance was exceptional, especially in mathematics and physics. Even his professors were amazed by his abilities.

"He enrolled in the Moscow Institute of Physics and Engineering, but the night seizures tormented him more and more, while during the day nothing seemed wrong.

"He suffered like this for eight years. He was in his third year of studies, and by then the seizures were happening almost three times every night, and his condition was worsening.

"His grandmother—my mother—shared our story with a nun at church. The nun asked if he had not received Communion in a long time. That's when we remembered that the seizures had started exactly when he stopped receiving Communion.

"The nun advised that he should go to Communion with faith. But he refused to even hear of it.

"We were living in a *dacha*[14] halfway to Zagorsk.[15] My sister and mother came to visit, to try and persuade him to go to church, but he stubbornly refused, didn't even want to hear the suggestion.

"His grandmother and my sister burst into tears, complaining that he didn't respect them at all. Eventually, he agreed to put on a clean shirt and prepare himself.

"It was Sunday morning. We barely made it in time for the train. We arrived in Zagorsk and found many young men and women there. He did everything we asked: he prayed with his whole soul, with warmth and sincerity.

"Our prayers, too, were fervent. He confessed to a young priest, received Holy Communion, and remained until the end of the Divine Liturgy. Then we returned home. My mother and sister went back to Moscow, and we stayed at the *dacha*.

14 A dacha is a country villa.

15 Zagorsk is a small town 70 kilometers north of Moscow. The largest ecclesiastical center of Russia, the Holy Trinity-Saint Sergius Lavra, is located there.

"Imagine our joy! From that day on, he didn't even move his head during the night. The seizures completely disappeared.

"And yet, before receiving Communion, he had three seizures every night, without exception. I myself, his mother, used to be afraid to even look at him during his fits.

"But now—blessed be the name of God—he is married, with two children, and everything has passed for good."

[32]

Miraculous Healing

The following incident is recounted by Fr. Dimitry Dudko himself:

"A woman from our parish—a medical doctor by profession—had been suffering for twelve years from stomach cancer. She vomited constantly and emitted such a terrible odor that it was very difficult for anyone to stay near her. She was on her deathbed.

"Her custody of her children had been revoked, she had been fired from her job, and her husband had abandoned her. Yet, she herself accepted her illness with humility and endurance, like a true Christian.

"In her final hours, she requested Holy Unction and Holy Communion. And the miracle happened!

"After the Unction was performed, and she received Holy Communion, the vomiting stopped, and little by little, the unbearable stench disappeared. The doctors confirmed, to their great astonishment, that she had been healed."

[32]

From the Mouth of the Leper

Saint Nicholas (Planas)

In the parish of Father Nicholas Planas (+1932), in a narrow alleyway, a leper in an advanced stage of the disease was living in hiding. His lips had been eaten away by the dreadful illness.

One day, the holy elder went to give him Holy Communion, but the man’s decayed mouth was unable to receive the Holy Body of the Lord, and the Divine Gift fell to the side.

Without the slightest hesitation, the saintly priest bent down, and with his own mouth, he received the Divine Pearl and consumed it—without suffering any harm.

As for the leper, he was eventually discovered by the authorities and was sent to the leper hospital.

[21]

Healing of the Woman with the Issue of Blood

The miracle that follows happened to a pious woman who suffered from frequent hemorrhaging, which prevented her from receiving Holy Communion. She was once advised to visit the charismatic elder, Fr. Hieronymos of Simonopetra (1871–1957), at the Church of the Ascension in Athens.

Saint Hieronymos of Simonopetra

She eagerly went and found him. It was during Great Lent.

"Prepare yourself to receive Communion on Holy Thursday," the elder told her.

"But what if I start bleeding again?" she asked.

"You go ahead," he replied, "and the sin will be on me."

After receiving Holy Communion, that woman never hemorrhaged again.

[28]

The Little Spoons and the Communion Spoon

There are Christians who are afraid to receive Holy Communion for fear of contracting germs! But if that were the case, none of the priests would be alive, since at the end of the Divine Liturgy they consume the contents of the Holy Chalice, from which hundreds of faithful—often with various illnesses—receive Communion.

And yet, not a single priest has ever suffered any harm. The Body and Blood of the Lord are "a consuming fire."

One of the many incidents that clearly prove this truth is the following:

When Metropolitan Panteleimon (Fostinis) of Chios (+1962) was a preacher in Attica, he once went to celebrate the Divine Liturgy at the "Sotiria" tuberculosis sanatorium.

There, the nurses brought him a large tray filled with many small spoons.

"Why did you bring these?" he asked them.

"The doctors told us," they replied, "to have you use a separate spoon for each patient—starting with the mildly ill and ending with the most seriously ill."

"These are not necessary," the priest replied with faith. "I have the Holy Spoon [*lavída*]."

Indeed, during the Divine Liturgy, he communed the patients in the usual manner, using the Holy Spoon, and afterward, he approached the Royal Doors to consume the remaining Gifts. He did this in full view of everyone so that the doctors would see and understand that Holy Communion is a fire that burns all things.

[10]

The Madman

A related incident also occurred in 1942 in Ioannina. The preacher Father Benedict Petrakis (+1961), after the Divine Liturgy at the small church of the Castle, went to the hospital there, which also housed the tuberculosis ward, to give communion to the sick.

A severely tubercular patient, as soon as he received communion, coughed up blood onto the sheet. Immediately, Father Benedict took it with the Holy Spoon, consumed it, and said to burn the sheet.

The doctors saw this and were terrified. "What is this madman doing?" they shouted. "Soon you will see him with galloping tuberculosis!"

But neither soon nor later did they see him with galloping tuberculosis. The grace of the mystery did not allow him to suffer anything.

[10]

Holy Communion Works Miracles

During the Great Lent of 1958, a priest visited the blessed Father Charalambos Vasilopoulos (+1982) in his cell at dawn.

"Please come with me," he says to him, "to the Saint Paul clinic, to hear the confession of and give communion to a sick man. I want him to get well for his relatives, who live far from the Church. Their minds are on money. No one is interested. Only the patient's fiancée is devout, and she wants him not to depart unprepared."

They went together to the clinic, performed the mystery of Holy Unction, and then Father Charalambos tried to hear his confession. Unfortunately, he was experiencing lapses of consciousness. Nevertheless, with difficulty, some rudimentary confession was made. Afterward, he gave him communion.

Well then, he got better! The Divine Communion worked its miracle. And on Thomas Sunday, he celebrated his wedding.

In 1959, one evening, Father Charalambos was called to visit a very refined elderly woman with heart disease, who lived below Lycabettus.

She had lived in Russia and then in Marseille, where she converted from Catholicism to Orthodoxy. Now she was 85 years old but did not want to receive communion. However, Father Charalambos brought the Immaculate Mysteries with him, in case he could persuade her. The doctor, as her family informed him, said she would certainly die that same night.

When he entered the house, and she saw him, she says to him: "I'm leaving."

"You're not going anywhere," he answers her. "I brought you the medicine. Do you have anything to tell me?"

Father Charalambos Vasilopoulos

She immediately confessed willingly and received communion.

After the Divine Communion, she took a turn for the better.

In the morning, they notified the doctor. "Didn't she die?" he wondered. When he visited her, he was amazed. He found that his medicines and science proved useless in the face of the power of Divine Communion.

Eventually, the elderly woman was healed and lived for another five years.

[10]

The Healing of a Small Child

Father Dimitrios Gagastathis (1902-1975) also recounts the following incident about the healing power of the Immaculate Mysteries:

"In August 1961, they brought a three-year-old child from the village of Ellinokastro who was very restless. The child would not calm down at all, day or night. He did not want to go to church. I celebrated the liturgy for his sake at the Church of the Archangels. However, he did not want to enter the church. He was shouting and crying loudly. They tied him to a church stall. Coming out for the Great Entrance, I passed over him with the Immaculate Mysteries. Immediately then he calmed down and slept until the end. After I gave him communion, he left peaceful and happy. Since then, his grandfather comes every year and has a liturgy celebrated at the Church of the Archangels."

[42]

The Skeptical Doctor

The blessed Dimitrios Panagopoulos (1916-1982), the divinely enlightened lay preacher, preached even at the Sotiria hospital, where others would not approach due to fear of tuberculosis.

Dimitrios Panagopoulos

There he was followed by the priest, Fr. Dimitrios Papantonis, who heard the confessions of the tuberculosis patients and celebrated the Divine Liturgy. One day, a doctor who had been following the talks with concern, approached the preacher and said to him:

"Mr. Panagopoulos, it is impossible for the priest to

consume the contents of the Holy Chalice. So many patients receive communion from it, and as is known, the tuberculosis bacterium is transmitted through saliva. So what does the priest do with the Body and Blood of the Lord that remains? Does he pour it into the disposal basin? But isn’t that a great sin?”

“Such a thing never happens,” countered the preacher. “Christ is not contaminated by bacteria. And there is no danger of infection from the Immaculate Mysteries.”

The doctor, however, could not believe it. Then this priest urged the doctor to attend the next Divine Liturgy, and at the end to stand somewhere so that he could see the priest’s movements at the time of consumption.

And so it happened. The doctor saw with his own eyes the celebrant consuming the contents of the Holy Chalice. He even saw him pour wine two or three times, taking care not to leave even a trace of the Body and Blood of the Lord.

From then on, the doctor not only believed, but also attended church and received communion together with the patients.

[27]

The Medicine of the Church

The blessed Archimandrite Eusebius Giannakakis (+1995), when he served as a parish priest at the Hippocration Hospital in Athens, experienced stunning miracles of healing patients through partaking of the Immaculate Mysteries:

A seriously ill patient, Mr. George F., had been in a state of aphasia for twenty days after a severe stroke. Professor

Goutas monitored him systematically because he had a high fever that reached 40 °C!

On the twenty-first day—something strange—the patient began to open his eyes and speak! The professor was puzzled. He thought the improvement would be temporary. However, the patient kept getting better, and in a few days, he was conversing comfortably and clearly.

Then the doctor spoke clearly about the medical perspective: "Dear Mr. George, your case was not amenable to any improvement, especially after such a high fever. Normally, you shouldn't be with us now."

"Professor," the patient calmly replied, "the supreme Physician, the Lord Jesus Christ, did not agree with you. The 'medicine' of the Church proves more effective. The hospital priest, after every Divine Liturgy, would willingly come to give me communion. I certainly couldn't speak, but I felt everything. And it seems the priest understood this, which is why he abundantly used the therapeutic means of our Church. The Body and Blood of Christ revitalize the soul and body. They heal even the greatest illnesses."

A woman, Mrs. Maria G., suffered from severe kidney failure. Her condition was steadily worsening.

One Saturday, the doctor found her with complete anuria. Leaving the hospital, he believed that by the next day his patient would have departed for eternity.

Later, however, the hospital priest visited her and suggested she turn to the heavenly Physician, the Lord Jesus Christ. She accepted with joy. She confessed sincerely, and on Sunday morning, after attending the Divine Liturgy, she partook of the Immaculate Mysteries. She received communion with ardent faith in the healing power of the Body and Blood of Christ.

And the miracle happened. After the Divine Communion, her face began to glow with health, and her urinary system started functioning normally.

The doctor could not believe it. After two or three days, having confirmed that she was completely healed, he allowed her to leave.

[12]

BIBLIOGRAPHY

1. Hieromonk Agapios (Landos), *The Salvation of Sinners*, ed. V. Rigopoulou, Thessaloniki 1993.
2. *Athonite Testimony* (periodical), published by the Holy Monastery of Xeropotamou, Mount Athos, vols. 8–9/1990, 12–13/1991, 16–17/1992.
3. *Saint Eugene of Trebizond*, published by the Holy Monastery of Paracletos, Oropos 1997.
4. *Saint John of Kronstadt*, published by the Holy Monastery of Paracletos, Oropos 1997.
5. *Saint Cyprian* (periodical), published by the Holy Monastery of Sts. Cyprian and Justina, Phylē, Attica, vols. 193–194/1985, 195–196/1985.
6. *Anagenissi* (Cretan newspaper), issue of 6/5/1991.
7. Anagnostopoulos, Spyros, *Athanasius of Agiou Lavra the Spiritual Father*, ed. "Simantro," Athens 1986.
8. Andrew of Mount Athos, Monk, *The Gerontikon of the Holy Mountain*, vol. A, 1992.
9. Anonymous hesychast, *Neptic Vision*, published by "Orthodox Hive," Thessaloniki 1979. In English: A Monk of Mount Athos, *The Watchful Mind*, (Yonkers, NY: St. Vladimir's Seminary Press, 2014), pp. 229-236.
10. Vasilopoulos, Charalambos, Archimandrite, *Miracles My Eyes Have Seen*, ed. "Orthodox Press," Athens, n.d. (no date).
11. Galanos, Mich., *The Lives of the Saints*, Apostolic Ministry of the Church of Greece, vols. A–D, Athens 1983.
12. Giannakakis, Eusebios, Archim., *Near to Pain and Together with the Afflicted*, Holy Monastery of St. John the Theologian, Aigio 1995.
13. Gouvalis, Daniel, Archim., *The Miracle of Faith*, Athens 1985.
14. *Frightening and Beneficial Stories*, Holy Monastery of Paracletos, Oropos 1995.
15. Fathers of the Holy Monastery of St. David, *A Holy Elder, the Blessed Father Iakovos*, Rovies, Euboea 1993.

16. *The Evergetinos*, vols. A–D, ed. Viktor Matthaiou, Athens 1957–1960.
17. Ioannis and Sophronios the Sophist, *The Ancient Leimonarion*, ed. Sot. Schoinas, Volos 1953.
18. *The History of the Monks of Egypt*, "Tinos" Publications, Athens 1992.
19. Ioannidis, Kleitos, *Contemporary Holy Elders*, Holy Monastery of St. Marina and St. Raphael, Xylotymbou, Nicosia 1995.
20. Kalliatso, Anargyros, *Father Porphyrius*, Orthodox Press, Athens 1993.
21. Martha, Nun, *Saint Father Nicholas Planas*, Astir Publications, Athens [1992].
22. Matthaiou, Viktor (ed. & publ.), *The Great Synaxaristes of the Orthodox Church*, vols. 1–14, Athens 1946–1950.
23. Meletios of Nikopolis, Metropolitan, *Father Joel*, Holy Metropolis of Nikopolis, Preveza 1994.
24. Melinos, Manolis, *Flowers of Holy Russia*, Athens [1995].
25. Moschos, Ioannis, *Leimonarion*, trans. Monk Theologos, Holy Monastery of Stavronikita, Mount Athos 1990.
26. Botsis, P., *Elder Hieronymos – The Hesychast of Aegina*, Athens 1991.
27. Boutsouris, Georg. & Vass., *Preacher Dimitrios Panagopoulos (1916–1982)*, Athens 1993.
28. Moses, Monk, *Hieronymos of Simonopetra – The Elder of the Ascension*, Holy Monastery of Simonos Petra, Mount Athos 1982.
29. Moses of Mount Athos, Monk, *The Blessed Elder Georgios Karslidis*, Holy Monastery of the Ascension of the Savior, Taxiarchai, Drama 1989.
30. Nicodemus of the Holy Mountain, *New Eklogion*, Astir Publications, Athens 1974.
31. Nicodemus (Bilalis), Monk, *Miracles of St. Athanasius the Athonite*, Holy Monastery of Great Lavra, Mount Athos – Athens 1991.
32. Dudko, Dimitrios, Presbyter, *Our Hope*, "He Elaphos" Publications, Athens 1979.

33. Xenos, Spyridon, Archim., *A Contemporary Saint*, Mount Athos 1987.
34. *The Shepherd* (periodical), published by the Holy Metropolis of Mytilene, vol. 2/1996.
35. *Orthodox Press* (newspaper, Athens), issue 30/4/1991.
36. *Saint Seraphim of Sarov*, Holy Monastery of Paracletos, Oropos 1996.
37. *Saint Sergius of Radonezh*, Holy Monastery of Paracletos, Oropos 1995.
38. Paisios of Mount Athos, Monk, *Saint Arsenius the Cappadocian*, Holy Hesychasterion of Evangelist John the Theologian, Souroti, Thessaloniki 1987.
39. Paisios of Mount Athos, Monk, *Athonite Fathers and Things Athonite*, Holy Hesychasterion of Evangelist John the Theologian, Souroti, Thessaloniki 1993.
40. Palladios [of Helenopolis], *The Lausiac History*, trans. Monk Symeon, Holy Monastery of Stavronikita, Mount Athos, 1990.
41. Papagathangelos Papastavrou, *Saintly Figures Who Sanctified Cyprus*, Nicosia 1988.
42. *Father Dimitrios Gagastathis*, "Orthodox Hive" Publications, Thessaloniki, n.d.
43. Papadopoulou, Styl., *The Blessed Iakovos Tsalikis*, Fathers of the Holy Monastery of St. David, Athens 1993.
44. Papanikolaou, Vasil., *Saint Savvas the New of Kalymnos*, Holy Monastery of All Saints, Kalymnos 1989.
45. Paschos, P. V., *The Spring of the Desert*, Akritas Publications, Athens 1985.
46. Paschos, P. V., *New Materikon*, Akritas Publications, Athens 1992.
47. [Petros, Hieromonk], *An Ascetic Bishop*, Holy Monastery of Paracletos, Oropos 1997.
48. Cyril of Scythopolis, *Life of Saint Euthymios the Great*, Evangelos Foundation "Saint John the Russian," Chalkida 1972.
49. Spetsieris, Joachim, Archim., *Memoirs*, vol. A (Mount Athos – Jerusalem), Athens 1931.

50. *Staretz Sampson*, Holy Metropolis of Nikopolis, Preveza 1991.
51. Tatsis, Dionysios, Presbyter, *Athonite Calendar*, Orthodox Press, Athens 1993.
52. Tsamis, D. G., *The Sinai Gerontikon*, Holy Monastery of the God-Trodden Mount Sinai, Thessaloniki 1988.
53. Tsamis, G. Dimitrios, *Materikon*, vols. B and C, "Saint Macrina" Brotherhood, Thessaloniki, 1991–1992.
54. Tsolakidis, Christos, *Messages from the Saints*, [Athens] 1995.
55. Chabakou, Theodora, Nun, *Gerontikon*, Lydia Publications, Thessaloniki 1993.
56. Charitidis, Leon. (trans.), *Saint Theodore of Sykeon*, "The Garden of the Virgin Mary" Publications, Thessaloniki 1987.
57. Chatzifotis, I. M., *The Church in the Struggle of the Forties*, "Atlantis" Publications, Athens [1982].
58. Cherouvim, Archim., *Sabbas the Spiritual*, Holy Monastery of Paracletos, Oropos 1995.
59. Cherouvim, Archim., *Daniel of Katounakia*, Holy Monastery of Paracletos, Oropos 1994.

UNCUT MOUNTAIN PRESS TITLES

Books by Archpriest Peter Heers

Fr. Peter Heers, *The Ecclesiological Renovation of Vatican II: An Orthodox Examination of Rome's Ecumenical Theology Regarding Baptism and the Church*, 2015

Fr. Peter Heers, *The Missionary Origins of Modern Ecumenism: Milestones Leading up to 1920*, 2007

Fr. Peter Heers, *Formation in the Love of Truth*, 2024

The Works of our Father Among the Saints, Nikodemos the Hagiorite

Vol. 1: *Exomologetarion: A Manual of Confession*

Vol. 2: *Concerning Frequent Communion of the Immaculate Mysteries of Christ*

Vol. 3: *Confession of Faith*

The Works of our Father Among the Saints, St. Hilarion (Troitsky)

Vol. 1: *On the Dogma of the Church: An Historical Overview of the Sources of Ecclesiology*

The Works of our Father Among the Saints, St. Raphael of Brooklyn

Vol. 1: *In Defense of St. Cyprian*

Vol. 2: *On the Steadfastness of the Orthodox Church*

Vol. 3: *Union with Rome?*

Other Available Titles

St. Gregory Palamas, *Apodictic Treatises on the Procession of the Holy Spirit*

Elder Cleopa of Romania, *The Truth of our Faith*

Elder Cleopa of Romania, *The Truth of our Faith, Vol. II*

Fr. John Romanides, *Patristic Theology: The University Lectures of Fr. John Romanides*

Demetrios Aslanidis and Monk Damascene Grigoriatis, *Apostle to Zaire: The Life and Legacy of Blessed Father Cosmas of Grigoriou*

Protopresbyter Anastasios Gotsopoulos, *On Common Prayer with the Heterodox According to the Canons of the Church*

Robert Spencer, *The Church and the Pope*

G. M. Davis, *Antichrist: The Fulfillment of Globalization*

Athonite Fathers of the 20th Century, Vol. I

Fr. Alexander Webster and Fr. Peter Heers, Editors, *Let No One Fear Death*
Subdeacon Nektarios Harrison, *Metropolitan Philaret of New York*
Elder George of Grigoriou, *Catholicism in the Light of Orthodoxy*
Archimandrite Ephraim Triandaphillopoulos, *Noetic Prayer as the Basis of Mission and the Struggle Against Heresy*
Dr. Nicholas Baldimtsis, *Life and Witness of St. Iakovos of Evia*
On the Reception of the Heterodox into the Orthodox Church: The Patristic Consensus and Criteria
Patrick (Craig) Truglia, *The Rise and Fall of the Papacy*
The Divine Service of the Eighth Œcumenical Council
The Orthodox Patristic Witness Concerning Catholicism
Hieromartyr Seraphim (Zvezdinsky), *Homilies on the Divine Liturgy*
Abbe Guettée, *The Papacy*
Fr. George Metallinos, *I Confess One Baptism*
Acts of the Eighth Œcumenical Council
George (Pachymeres), *Errors of the Latins* (2 volumes)
Miracles and Appearances of the Panagia

Select Forthcoming Titles

St. Hilarion (Troitsky), *Bible, Church, History: A Theological Examiniation*
Cell of the Resurrection, Mount Athos, *On the Mystery of Christ: An Athonite Catechism*
Fr. Theodore Zisis, *Kollyvadica*
St. Maximus the Confessor, *Opuscula: Theological and Polemical Works*
Fr. Peter Heers, *Going Deeper in the Spiritual Life*
Fr. Peter Heers, *On the Body of Christ and Baptism*
Athonite Fathers of the 20th Century, Vol. II

This 2nd English Edition of

MIRACLES AND REVELATIONS DURING THE DIVINE LITURGY

compiled by the Holy Monastery of the Paraclete, translated by Uncut Mountain Press, typeset in Baskerville, and printed in this two thousand and twenty fifth year of our Lord's Holy Incarnation is one of the many fine titles available from Uncut Mountain Press, translators and publishers of Orthodox Christian theological and spiritual literature. Find the book you are looking for at

uncutmountainpress.com

GLORY BE TO GOD FOR ALL THINGS

AMEN.